Beneath the Glitter

Bruce McGimsey

Henderson, Nevada
Ink & Quill Publishers
2015

Beneath the Glitter
Bruce McGimsey

Line/Content Editor: Denice Whitmore
Cover: Richard R. Draude
Interior Design: Jo A. Wilkins

ISBN: 978-1-934051-82-5/Paperback
ISBN: 978-1-934051-87-0/E-Pub

1. Biography & Autobiography/General
2. Biography & Autobiography/Personal Memoirs
3. Biography & Autobiography/Cultural Heritage

www.iqpublishers.com
Published and printed in the United States of America

Beneath the Glitter

He Made Her an Offer
She Couldn't Refuse

"Listen, mister, when I say jump through a hoop, you say, 'Light it on fire.' Do you understand me?"

"Yes, Dottie."

"Well then, let's hear you say it!"

"Light it on fire."

My former boss Dottie served in a dual capacity as swing shift hostess and queen bitch extraordinaire of the restaurant lounge I worked at on the Las Vegas Strip. I had gotten this busboy job two weeks earlier through my friend Tony, whose father owned the place. Per Tony and everyone else in my high school junior class, his father was in the mob. I had no way of knowing if this was true, but I did know the joint jumped twenty-four hours a day. They had lots of moneymaking slots along with a terrific restaurant business. Between that, the money the owners skimmed, and their rumored loan sharking business, the establishment seemed to manufacture gold. The owner, therefore, wanted a smooth-running place with no problems.

But he did have a problem, and her name was Dottie. In my brief sixteen years of life, I'd never before known a Dottie. For me, a typical awkward teenager, my most pressing thought was why doesn't anyone like me? Pre-Dottie, I knew a few females with nasty tendencies, maybe even a closet bitch here or there. I figured Dottie came out by her fifth birthday and honed her skills over the years to claim world-class status.

What made her so good was she loved loading the pistol. She was constantly agitating and pitting employee against employee by spreading rumors about who said what about whom. Unbeknownst to the owner, everyone hated Dottie. It wasn't until she mentioned the word "union" that he began to catch on.

It was the late sixties, and the unions had just started to organize the big hotel casinos, which had a terrible reputation for mistreating their employees. Ever so slowly, they were making progress, and no one wanted union problems.

Did that include this restaurant? Probably not, because the union had sweeter apples to pick. The thirty or forty employees at our establishment amounted to small potatoes compared to the casinos. But the owner didn't know that. So when Dottie started to organize our place, panic set in. She had worked in a union house back East for twenty years before moving to Vegas ten years ago. Besides being on a constant power trip, Dottie personified mean, vindictive, and cruel. The waitresses tipped her after every shift because they feared her. We had a restaurant manager, but he felt that the more Dottie worked, the less hassle he had to deal with.

Dottie figured on bringing a lot of union cards to the restaurant. Her favorite line was, "Once you sign a card, it'll take divine intervention to get fired." Per the National Labor Relations Board, it was unlawful to fire anyone for trying to organize a union. So now, do something wrong, and if management flips out, you just claim harassment because of your union activity. None of us knew any better. We just knew our hostess had become impossible, and this union threat made her invincible.

Personally, I never saw a union rep or had one solicit me, only Dottie. But what did I know? I just knew she resembled the Wicked Witch of the West, and everybody—staff, management, and clientele—despised her. And now, even the owner started second-guessing himself about Dottie's attitude.

The place verged on exploding. If the owner had simply consulted a labor lawyer, he would have found out how ridiculous unionizing this little joint sounded. But paying for a labor expert was out of character for this guy, so he dreamed up an alternative solution: he made her an offer she couldn't refuse. No, they didn't dump a horse's head into her bed or tell her that in one minute either her brains or her signature was going to be on that resignation slip. The owner, a Chicagoan, witnessed firsthand the kind of expense and hassle unions caused. Before this union scare and Dottie's insane power grab, the place seemed like a profit machine. Supposedly, the boss answered to his own people, so he conjured up another solution.

He told Dottie she no longer needed to come to work, and he'd pay her full salary, no strings attached. No more punching in or even coming in for her check.

"Listen, the situation could change some day and I'll expect you to come back, but your ten years of dedication has earned this." To stroke her a little more, he said, "I'll probably call you from time to time for consultation."

Dottie's instincts told her to watch out for a trick. She warned the owner that if she got fired or laid off because he no longer needed the position, the Labor Board would see right through it.

"No worries," the owner said. "The deal is foolproof, but you're smart to be suspicious. Have the Labor Board check out the contract."

Since the place was reputedly mob owned and run, you might be wondering, why not just whack her? Why not give her free burial service out in the mafia mortuary, otherwise known as the Las Vegas desert? Most of the employees wondered the same thing. But, if Dottie mysteriously disappeared, would the National Labor Relations Board make it their lifelong ambition to unionize this illicit little Mafia establishment to make a point? The owner reasoned, why gamble?

Sure enough, Dottie retired. This was simply too good to be true, both for her and for us. The place ran like aces without her. What a pleasure not being constantly yelled at. They replaced Dottie with a competent young lady who made me more tips. The tension eased as though a cloud had lifted and the restaurant relaxed again. The union threat disappeared even as it slowly ground away on the rest of the town.

Then, like hearing that the fat girl from two weeks ago was pregnant, bad rumors started surfacing. Someone spotted Dottie in the restaurant talking to the owner. This loony tune had the unmitigated gall to ask for a raise! Since she no longer received tips from the waitresses, she claimed she couldn't make ends meet. Call it Brazilian brass, call it temerity, or simply call it New York audacity. This gal never lacked nerve.

Because nobody wanted her back, the waitresses on shift volunteered to tip her daily, just as if she still worked there. The suggestion seemed to say, "Come in and collect five weekly envelopes for nothing, that's how much we hate you." Little did anyone know that a bigger problem loomed.

Dottie started thinking everyone liked her, and why not? The whole crew agreed to send her a weekly tax-free payoff. Dottie's thought process reasoned that the place really missed her and undoubtedly needed her expertise. In other words, she missed tormenting people and making them miserable. Even though she received a paycheck with tips for doing nothing but staying home, two months later she informed the owner she was coming back.

Neither the owner nor the employees knew what to do. The joint not only attracted a lot of casino staff, but also mobsters and wannabes, all notoriously excellent tippers. After she had left, the owner immediately noticed the difference in morale, but more importantly, the difference in the bottom line. Even though the restaurant's figures never matched the revenue from the other parts of the business, it still made him a fortune. Needless to say, nobody wanted a disruptive hurricane like Dottie blowing back into the restaurant, especially a whirlwind hoping to start the union threat again.

The owner came up with another solution. He offered her a promotion and a raise. She now received a new title as an assistant manager, overseeing the day shift in the restaurant—literally. The owner built a tower in the restaurant right over the cashier's booth, like a lifeguard's at the beach, only a lot taller, with a ramp for access.

She sat atop this tower and eyed the restaurant. She no longer greeted customers or directly interacted with employees. She saw which waitress got over-seated or what busboy was needed and where, and communicated with the hostess through a walkie-talkie. I likened her position to that of an offensive coordinator in a football game, who didn't stand on the sidelines at eye level but sat in a booth on top of the stadium, peering down to watch the plays unfold. This angle gave him a more objective view of the field, enabling him to call plays and adapt to what the defense did.

After this experience, I was convinced that a little eagle's nest atop a restaurant might be a perfect spot to manage from, not only for coordinating and directing the flow, but also for evaluating employees. In my later years, I tried to convince top-level brass that a tower could be an effective management tool. I received so much humiliating laughter that after my second try, I never mentioned it again.

What happened to Dottie? She came in and worked this job for a while, but unable to make people crazy, the job became boring. She no longer controlled the scheduling, the owner ordered her to tame her commands to the employees, and her new position limited her capacity to stir the pot. She hated it and tried like crazy to change her predicament. Bored stiff, she offered to trade jobs with the hostess for less money, but neither the owner nor the staff wanted that.

She finally backed herself into a corner with an either/or demand. She ended up quitting one day and, the next day, asking for her job back. She had become so delusional that she figured herself an invaluable asset to the restaurant. She even believed the crew would threaten to quit if she wasn't reinstated.

Once we knew for sure she quit, the whole crew, including busboys and dishwashers, met next door for a good-riddance party. Dottie had finally gotten her comeuppance.

Everyone knows the phrase, "There is no justice." In my life, I would say those words time and time again. In fact, I liken a little justice to that ever reclusive, super-rare, dove-crested purple-bellied African swallow. You hear it exists, other people tell grandiose stories of how euphoric it is to witness, but how many times do you ever see it? Well, on that day, I saw the swallow.

The Art of Dating

"Hey Bruce, Drabeck just went to the shower and I opened her curtains."

"Thank you, Myra!" I hung up the phone and turned to Jack, my new college roommate in the boys' dorm. "So, Jack, that looks like a very good telescope you've got there. How long would it take to put it together?"

Jack looked a little astounded. "Maybe a minute, but I haven't even unpacked. What's wrong with yours?"

"Yours looks a lot stronger than mine, and we're got about five minutes."

He set up the telescope. "Who's this Myra?"

I adjusted the eyepiece. "A friend in the girls' dorm. She likes me because I'm safe. I could go for her, but she's in love with her high school boyfriend, a big college jock just up the road at Utah State. She tags along with me, which keeps the guys off her, then does her jock every weekend. Okay, the queen has arrived. Ah, Linda! You will be mine, so help me God! Jack, check this unit out."

Not too reluctantly, Jack took his turn. "Jeez, you know this girl?"

"Only in my dreams, and even there I'm striking out."

"How are the women out here?" Jack said.

"In a year and a half, I've had two dates. I mean it's 1970, Woodstock, free love, the Age of Aquarius, and the best I can do is be Myra's safety valve." I noticed another of Jack's possessions. "What the hell is that thing?"

"A radio I'm building. I like to tinker with electronics."

Linda Drabeck slipped into a flannel nightgown and off

went the lights. But on this night, luscious Linda played second chair to my new roommate. We roomed on the eighth floor of a fourteen-story men's dormitory. The room paralleled the three women's dorms about two hundred yards away. With my telescope—and, for that matter, everyone else's—the best we could do was to see images. Now, this puppy that Jack brought allowed us to read the letters on a Coke carton in the back of Linda's room. But telescopes now amounted to a mere side attraction. My mind churned at warp speed. I foresaw a plan to lift myself and my new best friend Jack out of dorm-rat obscurity and into coed heaven.

"Tomorrow you'll meet Myra. By the way, do you have any larceny in you?"

The next day, we sat with Myra at lunch.

"Jack, can you really do that?" Myra asked.

"You get me that girl's radio and I'll take care of the rest."

"Okay, I'm in, let's do it Friday," Myra said. "There's a candle-lighting downstairs in the mezzanine. That'll keep every girl in the dorm busy for at least an hour."

"What the hell is that?"

"When a girl gets engaged, everyone gets together and passes a lit candle around a room. Sooner or later the lucky girl blows out the candle and we all gush with envy and admiration. Kind of sickening. It'll be easy, long as you get it done in an hour."

Friday night, Myra delivered the clock radio to Jack's van just like she promised. The radio belonged in Cindy and Lisa's room. That these two golfers from San Luis Obispo were the most popular girls in the dorms was no coincidence. Myra picked them because the other girls gathered in their room like antelope to a watering hole. They weren't just well liked; the whole dorm trusted them, and they commanded the kind of friends the other coeds confided in.

Ten minutes later, Jack finished putting a listening device into the radio and kicked off my plan to find out exactly what went on in a girl's head. Myra snuck the radio back in with no problem.

Thus, in my young life, this marked the end of my age of

innocence and officially started my new college career. I will never admit that this represented the high point of my life, I possess way too much pride for that. But this had to be the funniest, most ear-popping, eye-opening, consistent giggle-fest I ever encountered.

The room Myra picked out for us bubbled with nonstop energy. Sometimes a few girls, sometimes lots of girls. Guys thought about girls a lot, and we talked about women constantly. Occasionally we did have other conversations, like about sports, drugs, the current war, and on occasion, even our studies. The girls on the other hand seemed to talk about guys exclusively. Well, maybe except for clothes. Sometimes, depending on who the visiting girls were, they even got a touch raunchy. They talked a lot about sex and the perils of sex. Most amazing, they kept a mental dossier on just about every guy in the dorms, including me. The truly spectacular thing was that my band of brothers and I garnered some interest.

I no longer guessed at who to take out because Myra made a point to ask every available girl her opinion of me. Our friendship didn't seem to make anyone suspicious of Myra because once she steered the conversation in our direction, she'd leave the room, and the talk about guys would go on unimpeded. We not only knew who was interested, but how we did on our date—too aggressive, not aggressive enough.

Even more fun, I earned myself a new nickname, "the Cat." The bug enabled me to inform my friends which girls they should ask out. For instance, when I told Bill he'd be guaranteed success if he asked Jamie out, he asked, "How do you know?"

"Hey, who's the Cat?"

Not every girl in the dorms walked through this room, but the goings-on of who dated whom certainly came up very frequently within those four walls. What went on in the girls' dorm always got hashed out in the Spy Room, as we dubbed it. God Bless Myra!

My inner circle and I dated girls who'd never seemed interested, or so we thought. Before, I was clueless. Now I had an awesome edge. Just listening to a girl's thought process boggled the mind. They controlled the direction of a date from the get-go, the things they expected, the reactions they hoped for, what to do and say, and when to do it or say it. We figured the only way to get caught was to tell someone outside the High Command. The High Command consisted of Jack, Myra, and me. So we never did.

How often in your life have you had a conversation with your significant other that went like this?

He: "Are you mad? Did I do something wrong"?

She: "Well, if you don't know by now, I'm not going to tell you."

Now I knew beforehand and corrected the situation. I pro-acted in situations instead of reacted. On a typical first date I would say, "Janet, I hope you had a good time. I'll let you absorb this night and call you in a few days. But be prepared, I will be asking you out again." Then I would hightail it back to my dorm and tune in on the night's proceedings in the Spy Room. If Janet wasn't close to the golfers' room, Myra would entice her there for a chat.

"Hey Janet, come down to Cindy's room, we've got soda and snacks." (I would buy the goodies, but Myra would take the credit.) "How'd the date go? Did he make a move?"

"No, there were too many jocks down in the lobby."

"Is he gonna ask you out again?"

"He said he'd call in a few days. How come you've always got snacks? Doesn't this get expensive?"

"Myra buys all this junk." Cindy said. "Where do you think Bruce will take you next?"

"Someplace intimate, I hope."

Music to my ears.

It was also always a kick to find out about a guy's ineptness. I'm talking about the cool guys and those who thought they deserved feather beds, especially the jocks. Just imagine the fun in hearing what girls really thought of some of these jerks who fancied themselves God's gift to women. Sometimes they'd reiterate some goofy comment a guy made on a date, trying to be suave. The girls laughed hysterically retelling their story. Girls told girls, who told other girls. So, this idiot jock became a laughingstock and never knew it. What a sense of euphoria it gave me to watch these nimrods strut around campus.

There was one jock, a baseball player, who particularly made my ass ache because he always seemed to be in my face every time I went to the girls' dorm. This guy could hit and reportedly was the one guy on our college team who had a shot at the majors. So one night as we glued our ears to the listening device, we hear the girls mention this idiot. It turns out this fabulous hitter expected special service from his dates. He wasn't after the normal things the rest of us typical guys wanted. No, he expected the girls to caress and fondle him. Apparently he demanded this from his dates and felt it should be a girl's pleasure because of who he was.

On the rarest of occasions, our choices are limited, and in this instance, I felt circumstances dictated my next move. After we quit laughing, I felt my one and only choice in response to the best hitter on the team was to nickname this guy the "master batter." The next day, via Myra, the nickname spread through the dorms like mono. He'd walk by a table full of girls at lunch and you could read their lips as they mouthed the word master batter and then broke out laughing. At the baseball games, every time he stepped up to the plate, you'd hear something like "Okay, Master Batter, give it a ride!" College kids can be so cruel.

The fun little experiment backfired with one girl I dated. Because of the Spy Room, I started to fancy myself a player. For the most part, this never seemed to be a problem. College attracted a lot of self-indulgent men looking to take advantage. I think most coeds came to expect it, and a lot of women tolerated this little character flaw, while some gals even enjoyed it.

But not Pamela. Pamela was a freshman my junior year and an absolute head-turner. When you looked at Pamela, you always looked again. A farm girl from a small town in Wyoming, shy and reserved, she dressed a little conservatively and maybe a little hick. Nonetheless, the jocks fired at her constantly. Every time you saw her, she was surrounded by these creeps. After a few months, my homeboys and I just assumed her off-limits. Until one fateful night, when she walked into the Spy Room. Trooper Myra immediately started grilling her.

11

"Are you interested in the jocks?"

"Not at all. Once you're nice to any of 'em, they hang like flies. Nobody else will come near you."

"I know someone you might like, he's real funny."

"What's he look like and how do I meet him?"

"No problem," Myra said, "just sit with me at dinner, and I promise he'll come around to investigate." About twenty minutes later, Myra gave me the thumbs up at the window, knowing I both watched and, of course, listened. The next night at dinner, I asked Pamela out.

The formula Myra and I worked out had already been tried and tested. With my secret weapon, Pamela succumbed almost helplessly and became smitten within a few dates. That, I'm afraid, amounted to the only glitch in the plan.

I liked Pamela because she always laughed at my attempted humor, and for as good as she looked, she always remained unbelievably nice. But for a twenty-year-old guy just beginning to exercise his raging hormones, I wanted lust, not love, and so Pamela figured to be just another conquest to up my kill ratio.

I did what all self-centered, lustful college guys do. I manipulated her feelings and toyed with her emotions until I got what I wanted. She looked so good, and having her as my arm piece stroked my ego. But when I quit her, I didn't just ease out of seeing her, I let her go like a popcorn fart in a hurricane. I became cruel and insensitive. Because of my lack of character, I broke an angel's heart. I never really put it all into context until I heard her crying one night in the Spy Room while her friends commiserated. Even Myra despised me for my heartless cruelty.

I took a hard look at myself and hated what I saw. The Spy Room had turned me into a monster, or so I rationalized. Hell, I liked this girl. I just got caught up with my own self-absorption. I figured a lesson needed to be learned here.

Some girls in the dorms felt I deserved not just a lesson, but a sharp poke in the eye. Granted, this experience humbled me, and for the rest of the year I tried to be nice to Pam, even though she no longer felt in the mood. Nonetheless, I tried to be pleasant to her and she was civil to me. But some of the other girls felt I had some brutal payback coming. Fortunately for me, the Spy Room warned me of any adverse plans, so for the rest of the year I avoided the traps they set.

From then on, I swore never to do this again. Did it mean taking a vow of celibacy? Hell, no! Did it mean I needed to be sorry for invading the privacy of others? Again, hell no! Did it mean I would ask Jack to dismantle the listening device in the spy room and stop this foolishness? Are you out of your freaking mind!?

But I swore never to purposely toy with a girl's feelings just to satisfy my carnal desires, and all in all, I believe I fulfilled that pledge. On the other hand, for anyone just starting their dating experience, I highly recommend a listening device. Because I'm here to tell you, that was sure fun!

Hitchin' to Vegas

"Okay, Bruce, one more month and we can kiss Weber State College goodbye. Once I graduate, I ain't ever coming back. Besides, I need the money. Let's do it."

"Are you kidding?" I asked Dave. "We've got one week of spring break, and you gotta figure two days to hitch to Vegas and two days back to Ogden. I mean, do they even pick up hitchhikers in Utah?"

"Two days, are you nuts? We'll make it down there in half a day. I've hitchhiked a dozen times and never had a problem. It's easy—two clean-cut guys like us? Hell, we'll get Jack to drop us off at the freeway on-ramp, and within fifteen minutes, we'll catch our first ride."

"I don't know, Dave, I haven't got much of a stake to gamble on."

"Neither do I, that's why we're going to make a little money. I'm feeling lucky."

"All right, but I'm not going to spend all day out on the freeway ramp. If nothing happens in two hours, I'm quitting and heading right back home."

There are a lot of do's and don'ts when you hitchhike. I'm not going to bother listing them all as I tell this story. But I am going to mention one big don't, which undoubtedly trumps all other don'ts. So, pay attention, this one is very important.

When hitchhiking, do not hitch with a great big giant six-foot-four, four-hundred-pound man. Call it profiling, call it bias against horizontally challenged people, but I promise, if you team up with a guy who will single-assedly consume the whole back seat, motorists tend to pass on offering you rides.

Yup, Big Dave was a doughnut short of four hundred pounds, and I'm not talking a tight four hundred. No, sir, Dave carried around a lot of excess blubber. If you put on one of his shirts, you felt like a small pole holding up a big tent. When we hit the freeway, people not only skipped looking at our LAS VEGAS OR BUST sign, they focused solely on this oversized freak of nature.

Three hours passed, and I'd had enough hitchhiking. We stood out on the on-ramp, and then later on, right out on the side of the freeway and never even got a nibble. No sooner am I ready to stop our adventure when an old, faded, green Ford pickup cuts across three lanes and screeches to a halt about twenty yards ahead of us. Then this old banger gets flipped into reverse, smoking the tires as it backs up. With the truck parallel to us, the driver pushes the passenger door open.

"Hurry," he screams, "get in! I need a big favor."

We get in, sidestepping a case of beer on the floorboard. He floors it before we even get the door closed.

"Help yourself to a beer. I doubt if I'll get to 'em all."

"Oh, I don't know," I say, "I count at least six empties."

"Oh no, guys, have one while they're still cold."

"I'd rather keep my hands empty," Dave says, "I might need them to help keep me from crashing through the windshield. Aren't you going a little fast?"

"This is where I need the favor. I just had six Indian bucks flip me off and chuck beer cans at me. I can't take 'em alone but I figure with you two, we can kick some ass."

"Maybe if we live," Dave says, "but weaving in and out of traffic at ninety per has got me flinching six times a minute. You're inches away from hitting someone."

"Yeah, I know, big guy, but if I don't speed up, I won't catch them."

"At least you're not all caught up in the seat belt craze."

"Hell no, took 'em out, don't believe in 'em."

Dave looks down at my right foot. "How's your floor brake working?" My foot was jammed to that imaginary brake we all use when we want the driver to slow down.

"I think the pads are shot."

16

"Hey, Cowboy," Dave says, "what did you say they were driving?"

"Blue sixty-four Chevy. You see them?"

"Looks like them up there on the right."

I look at Dave in amazement that he's willing to put us right in the middle of this jackpot.

Dave looks at me and whispers, "If he stops, we can get out and run."

Why were we calling him Cowboy, you might ask. Simple, there were signs: the bits of hay in the old truck's bed, the expensive cowboy hat this guy wore, and the dozen beers he'd downed were definite clues. On top of all that, we were chasing Indians with three rifles on his rack in the back window.

"Guys, hand me down that thirty-aught on the top rack. I got no ammunition, but they won't know that. I'll pull up on their side and see if I can't scare 'em into pulling over."

Here we are on the freeway going ninety. The cowboy has one hand on the steering wheel and the other on a rifle, hanging out the window yelling obscenities. Then, like a B-movie from Hollywood, the Indians pulled out their own shotgun. Everyone knows to bring bullets to a gunfight, unless of course you're an idiot cowboy.

He backed off in a hurry and turned onto the Lehigh off-ramp just before Provo, Utah, and about six miles down the street, he found a place to buy ammunition. We hid behind a bush in a field while he drove up and down the street searching for us. The crazy bastard honestly thought we wanted to help him.

Our problem now was how to get back to the freeway and start hitchhiking again. By the time we got there, we only had about another hour of daylight. For whatever reason, nobody picks up hitchhikers at night. If we could get to the Brigham Young University campus, we could probably crash at one of the boys' dormitories.

As it happened, a little old man picked us up. As we piled in his car, he informed us that he couldn't take us to Vegas but would drop us on an off-ramp on the other side of Provo. When we suggested that we preferred the BYU campus, he asked if we played pool. He introduced himself as Bill and took us to

17

one of the three bars in the Provo area, promising that, when we finished, he'd gladly drop us off at any one of the dorms.

When we walked into the tavern, pretty much everyone in this crowded little joint started hooting and hollering. The comments ranged from "Two more suckers, huh, Bill?" to "Hey, fellas, this guy's a hustler." No sooner do we get back to the pool table than this guy asks us if we played one-pocket. Nobody plays one-pocket.

In this game, whichever pocket you made your first ball in, you were then obligated to make the rest of your balls in the same pocket. So the game usually played at a slow, tedious pace, chock full of strategy. To win, you probably were going to have to bank some key shots. Now it all made sense. This was One-Pocket Willy, the best one-pocket player in the state. Every year he won half a dozen one-pocket tournaments in the area. Take him out of this form of pool and into eight ball or nine ball, and Willy turned into a mediocre player.

But in his bar, in his town, with him having the car, we stuck to his game. I played first for a dollar a game which seemed to be his standard hustle. He easily won the first three games, let me win the fourth game, and then offered to raise the bet to ten dollars a game. My pool skills were limited, but my partner's abilities figured about three levels up from mine.

Big Dave ranked locally as one of the top ten nine-ball players in the state. When a four-hundred-pound man plays run-out nine-ball, a bigger-than-life reputation usually follows. Dave held this kind of repute.

When Dave jumped up to accept Willy's bet, almost everyone in the bar took notice. Dave not only played well, but he played a little flashy and liked showing off. On top of that, he got a little lucky. He beat Willy out of twenty dollars in about ten minutes which shocked most of the patrons. This in turn infuriated Willy.

"Hey, Willy, the kid took you off like a rocket launcher. I've never seen you lose before."

With a little added gloating from Big Dave, when it came time for our ride to the campus, Willy told us, "I ain't giving you smartasses shit. You can walk for all I care."

That's just great. Dave's showing off had won us twenty

more dollars, but now we were forced to sleep in a field across from the bar. We succumbed to a tough night, which proceeded into an even tougher morning. Walking to the freeway on-ramp took us two hours, and we stood there another three hours begging for rides. Just when all seemed lost, up pulls a big semi-truck and the driver tells us he's on his way to Vegas, hop in. As I jumped up first and crawled to the middle, this nice, pleasant man about thirty said, "Wow, you look tired, go ahead and lay out in the bunk. I'll let you know when we get there." All right, we finally caught a break. Things were looking up.

A good four and a half hours later, I sit up, completely refreshed, take a quick gander at our desert surroundings, and surmise our location approximately seven miles outside of St. George, Utah. Meaning, our estimated time of arrival in Vegas was about two hours away. I leaned forward and said, "This is progress."

No sooner had I said that, when Big Dave says, "What? You think you can whip my ass! You must be hallucinating from all that gas Bruce was passing awhile back."

"Hallucinating, my ass! I'll tell you what, fat boy, you keep this up and I'll tap dance on your over-proportioned head."

"Well, listen, I usually don't beat someone senseless unless it's worth my while."

"Okay, big boy." The truck driver slammed his fist on the steering wheel. "I'll bet you and your friend twenty dollars each."

"How do we know you'll pay us once you're slithering around on the ground screaming for Mommy?"

"Trust me, boys, if a buffet-eatin', Pepsi-drinkin' slob kicks my ass, you can have the extra key to my semi. I'll put the money in a hide-a-key container underneath my rig."

So, the next thing I know, instead of heading for Vegas in an air-conditioned truck traveling at sixty-five per, we've pulled over onto a side ramp underneath an overpass. It's a hundred and seven degrees and these two knuckleheads are headed around a hill preparing to duke it out. All for the simple pleasure of winning forty dollars and the knowledge one of them was tougher than the other. I asked Dave if he figured that either way, we'd lose our ride, and if this seemed perfectly rational to him.

"Sure, we'll lose our ride," he said, "but we'll get another ride no problem, and the extra money is bound to come in handy. Besides, this guy needs a little lesson in humility."

No sooner do these two idiots square off, it begins to look bad for Big Dave. The truck driver kept slipping and ducking Dave's looping right hand. I'd never seen anyone duck punches. Every time Dave threw a right hand, this guy slipped the punch and hit him in the kidneys. Take a four-hundred-pound man in one-hundred–plus-degree weather, add about a dozen kidney shots, and I think you can pretty well kiss your wager goodbye. Dave had slowed down to a walking crawl. But he'd been in a lot of fights, so he mustered up one last move. He threw a jab and faked a right hand, which the truck driver went for. With our friend's left hand out of defensive position, Dave mustered the biggest right-hand haymaker I'd ever seen.

Now I'm here to tell you, when this punch landed, it sounded like a stick breaking in two instead of a fist crushing a jawbone. This guy's knees shook in a delayed reaction. It seemed to take a full three seconds before he went down for the count, and that was that. While he listened to his bell ring and did the dry tuna dance on the ground, I couldn't help but throw him one last shot.

"Well, buddy," I said, "that just goes to show you, it ain't over till the fat guy swings."

Cute line, the big guy loved it, but as it turned out, the spare hide-a-key container contained nothing but a key, less forty dollars, and it didn't fit any of the truck's doors. We finally assumed it was for his personal car back wherever he lived.

We now faced an eight-mile walk to St. George, Utah, in scorching hot weather. Dave was perfectly willing to pick a fight with a guy and beat the living crap out of him, but when I suggested we check his wallet for the money he owed us, Dave says, "Oh no, that's like stealing." Thus we each weighed in twenty dollars lighter, and worst of all, as we walked on the freeway, the truck driver snuck up on us and about blew our ears off with some sort of fog horn. He flipped us the standard truck driver salute.

"Hey, stick it back in your nose, it looks better!"

We arrived in St. George around midnight and caught a bus to Vegas. I was so tired I went straight to the back row of seats and lay out on the floor. At the time, no one sat in those three seats. Four hours later, I woke up to a girl's bare feet in my face. She held a baby in her arms and apologized, but said I appeared to be in such a deep sleep my friend told her not to wake me up, her feet wouldn't bother me. Thank you, Dave.

Here's the rub. With all the problems we encountered hitchhiking, how could I enjoy myself in Vegas knowing I faced the same hassles hitching back, especially since we lost every gamble we tried? Even playing on scared money, we all but busted out in two days. So far, the high point of our trip was a midget, or dwarf, inviting us to a fabulous hotel party in one of the mega-suites. But that's another story.

Okay, here we are out on the freeway, thumbs out with our standard SLC sign, which of course stood for Salt Lake City. I swear, it seemed people looked right through us. So I decided on a new approach. I crossed out the SLC with a single line through it and wrote underneath it in big bold letters, FREE ADVICE.

Besides all the laughs, we caught a ride in ten minutes. This one shook out so well, even Dave couldn't blow it. An old Mormon couple bought us lunch and gave us a ride all the way back to Provo, seventy miles from our final destination, Ogden, Utah. The big question we faced was do we ask them to drop us off at the college campus to guarantee shelter for the night? Or do we gamble that with one hour's worth of daylight and expect my new free-advice sign to create one more magical ride? We chose the latter and struck out.

Now here we are, out on a freeway ramp at dusk weighing our apparent two options. Start walking to the campus, or hang out awhile and end up sleeping in the desert opposite the freeway. Lo and behold, like an angel appearing to us from atop a mountain, up drives good old One-Pocket Willy. As I live and die, Willy pulls up and says, "Hop in, fellas. Let's play some pool."

Right off, he admits he made a few phone calls and had compiled a complete dossier on Dave's game. He said when a guy tips the scales at record levels, a certain reputation follows him around. He promised no hard feelings. Win, lose, or draw, he'd drive us back to the college once the action subsided. To us, a bar sounded better than a dry gulch in the desert. Maybe we could win back all the money we lost in Vegas.

"Listen, boys," Willy said, "I get tired of cruising the freeway, hustling hitchhikers out of dollar bills just to make ends meet. Once in a while I like to get down and play."

Our total stake to gamble amounted to sixty dollars. Dave held forty, and I managed to save twenty, either for emergency or a bet we just had to wager. When we walked in, it appeared word had spread about our previous encounter with Willy, because the match generated a lot of interest. Willy insisted on playing one-pocket, and since Dave won so easily the first time around, we thought, why not?

We jumped right out of the gate playing for twenty a game and got nowhere, exchanging the same twenty dollars for the next two hours. Finally, Willy broke through and beat Dave out of his forty dollars. But when we asked for our ride to the campus, Willy refused. Apparently, he needed to bust us for the sake of his pride, and he wanted my last twenty. So, he offers to pay us two-to-one on my last twenty. If we win one game, we would get back to even, and after that game, he promised we'd get our ride.

How could we refuse? It took Willy about four minutes to take that last twenty. His true nature now jumped out at us. He started gloating to the bar how he just busted the smartasses, and to show everyone what a good sport he was, he would take the last twenty-dollar bill he'd won, set it on fire, and light his victory cigar with it. He then proceeded to do it. On top of that, he lifted his glass to everyone in the tavern "This calls for a sociable. Let's everyone raise our glasses to the zinger I just handed these two punks. Boys, no need to be bad sports. If you had any money left, I'd take that from you too."

"Wow, Willy, that's pretty good zinging," I said, "but how about a chance to win our money back?"

"You still have money left? What's the wager?"

"I'll bet you with that fresh pack of cigarettes in your shirt pocket, I can take one of the cigarettes and set it up on an ashtray so that one end touches the table and one end sticks up above the ashtray. Then, I'll hit the top end of that cigarette, flip it up making it do at least two complete turns in the air tiddlywinks style, and land it on top of your pack of cigarettes."

"How much?" Willy said.

I looked at Dave, now in complete bewilderment, and said, "You got any money?"

"Yeah, a quarter."

"Willy, bet you a quarter."

"Smartass, you've got a bet."

I set the pack up so that a three-cigarette pronged V stood halfway out of the pack. Sure enough, Willy said, "Oh no, the way you've got it set up, I could do that."

"Okay, Willy, bet you a quarter you can't."

So, he tried it and never came close. He then slid the quarter over to me and said, "This, I gotta see. If you can beat me out of another quarter, then more power to you."

I took a few minutes setting everything up perfectly, hamming it up as best I could. Now, with the whole bar completely focused on me, I raised my open palm to about eye level, then, with all the force I could muster, slammed it down on the whole pack, smashing it into a hundred little pieces, the only whole cigarette left being the tiddlywinks one supposedly doing the flips.

"Oops, I missed. Here's your quarter, Willy."

The bar exploded with laughter. The whole joint found this hilarious, with one exception. Willy looked like he wanted to kill me.

So, I said to everyone in the tavern, "To show all of you what a good sport I am, I'm going to take this perfectly good personal check, write it for a hundred dollars, set it on fire and light this last victory cigarette with it." One-Pocket immediately started swearing at me. What could I say? I announced to the place that I wanted to raise my glass for a sociable. "Folks, let's tip our glasses to that famous old yogism, 'It ain't over till the smartass zings.'"

We set our glasses down, gave One-Pocket Willy the high hat, and walked outside. One of the patrons followed us outside and offered us a ride back to Ogden. Ah, yes, life was sweet after all.

The High Road

So here we are in a casino buffet in Vegas, half starved, looking to eat everything in sight. We've hitched down to Vegas over spring break and we're losing at everything we try. Now, right there in the buffet line, this little guy starts talking to us.

"Gee, you're a big son of a bitch, how much do you weigh?"

"Not that much really," Dave says, "I just look big next to you. How tall are you?"

"Four foot two. Lookit, fellas, my name's Joey, why don't you guys come eat with me? I've got a party I want to invite you to."

"I'm Bruce, and the big son of a bitch you just insulted is Big Dave. Let's hear about the party."

"My friend Scotty is tossing up a bash in one of the suites. He's a little person like me, and you're going to meet every Hollywood dwarf you've ever seen in a movie."

His face finally registered. "I thought I recognized you. I've seen you on TV. Is this party going to be all little people?"

"Oh no, there'll be a bevy of beautiful Hollywood wannabes up there. You'll recognize some of them from bit parts, but none of them have hit the big time, not yet."

"Okay, I'll bite," I said. "How do you get them to come?"

"We lead them to believe that we know big-time producer types who can jumpstart their careers."

"So do you?"

"Hell, no, we're not big stars, we just bang out a living. That's why you didn't know my name. But they don't know that for sure, and since they see us on the screen once in a while, they figure we must know someone."

25

Bruce McGimsey

"Where do we come in?" Dave asks.

"First off, you're so big it'll be a kick me walking in with you. Then I'm going to introduce you guys as first-time moviemakers fresh out of film school. I'll tell them you're putting together an independent film and you're looking for new talent."

"Are they gonna buy this?"

"They can't afford not to. In this game you follow every lead like it's the career maker. If it doesn't pan out, at least they drink for free. They have nothing better to do anyway. Trust me, there are going to be a thousand guys up there trying to sell them a bill of goods, and every once in a while somebody is legit."

"I've got to ask, why do you need us? I mean we don't know anything about moviemaking."

"Because it just so happens I'm desperate. One of the wannabes is my girlfriend. I love her, and better yet, I know she loves me, but I kind of backed myself into a corner. When I first met her, I strung her along like I could put her with the right people and help her career. For her, career comes before love. Now I'm trapped. She wouldn't have showed up tonight if she didn't think she was going to meet some big shot."

"You must know a few people in Hollywood."

"We all do. We just don't have the juice to make it happen. That kind of pull is reserved for big stars. But if I didn't lead her on, I never would have gotten this far with her. I never figured she was going to fall in love with me. So now I'm east of the rock and west of the hard place."

Understand, at best we figured Joey might be a little cute to women, but a beautiful starlet type falling in love with him seemed like a real stretch. So Dave asks with a suspicious and even wry smile, "Are you sure she's in love with you?"

"Wait till you see the way she acts around me. So what do you think, you guys in?"

"I'm in, how about you, Dave?"

"Nothing to lose. If we blow it, we'll just leave and never see these people again."

Joey had no idea how lucky he'd gotten when he picked us to engineer this charade. Maybe hitchhiking back to Weber State was going to be the challenge of our young lives, but

26

acting like big shots amongst a room full of heart stoppers played right into my wheelhouse. I could muster up creative talking—i.e. bullshit—like nobody I knew. Truth be known, even at my young age, I fancied myself a master.

Ten minutes later, we arrived at the party. The suite consisted of four bedrooms, two bathrooms, a kitchen, and a living room with a built-in bar and a small swimming pool. About fifteen to twenty drunken little dwarfs scurried about doing things you always imagined dwarfs did when they drank. They played keep-away with purses, slapped girls asses, and best of all, set up a swing over the pool, and every so often one would do the Tarzan yell and splash into the water. This party played out like a stereotypical midget movie except of course there were a million girls.

So how does an upstart writer describe the euphoria that two college kids felt being introduced as two filmmakers to a room full of gorgeous Hollywood hopefuls? Simply put, I don't posses that type of writing skill. Nope, the most appropriate thing to do here is to offer up my deepest and most sincere thanks to the guy who invented breast implants. I salute you, whoever you are. On top of that, Joey gave us credibility by dropping names of people whom we supposedly knew, just enough so these voluptuous tarts took us seriously despite their natural distrust from previous ruses.

After mingling awhile, we both honed in on our potential conquests with our only real problem being when to turn off the BS. Let's face it, how often do kids get to play kings for the night? On occasion, Joey would reel us in a little and give me that look, you know, the eyebrow squint when someone tries to tell you you're going too far.

So picture Dave and me on a sofa with three girls squeezed in between us and an absolute head turner sitting on my lap. Opposite us is another couch with four more knockouts and one little male weasel constantly trying to shoot holes in our act, questioning my legitimacy every time I talk. There's always one. Between the couches is a coffee table, and at the head of the table a matching armchair with this exotic-looking babe trying her best to be a part of our conversation.

This was Susan, Joey's big heartthrob. Joey gave us explicit instructions to focus on Susan and convince her that we showed up strictly to meet her because of his diligence. That's exactly what we tried to do, but let's face it, temptation abounded.

"So, Susan," I said, "it comes down to this. Can you act?"

"What do you care if she can act, I'm the one sitting on your lap."

With a wink to my new Hollywood vixen, I said, "It doesn't matter if you can act, you're going to earn a role in our movie later on tonight," which of course led to hoots and catcalls.

Dave asks, "Susan, how're your improvisational skills?"

"They're great, let me show you."

Now Joey comes over, having fetched Susan a drink. "Hey, Joey, thanks for getting me the drink. Go ahead and set it on the table, then come over and sit on my lap, you little cutie."

We'd been looking for some display of affection from her toward Joey, but so far nothing, so he relished this opportunity. First thing, she started rubbing Joey's shoulders.

Joey sighed and rolled his eyes. "Ah yes, you're hired." He then looked at us as like, I told you she loved me.

Susan slid one hand under his armpit and started rubbing his chest, and with the other, began gently squeezing his neck right beneath both of his earlobes. Now Susan asks, "So, Joey, who's your favorite Hollywood personality?"

"John Wayne, of course, who else?"

"You got any funny stories about The Duke?"

"I've got a great story."

As Joey tells the story, Susan moves her lips while squeezing his neck, making it look like she's a ventriloquist and Joey is the dummy sitting on her knee. People smile and then laugh, and Joey believes they're laughing at his story. Susan worked this like a vaudeville act. Laughter eventually turned into hilarity because of Susan's impeccable timing. Sometimes she'd strain her face as if some words were harder to say with her mouth closed.

"Joey, what's the funniest story you got?" Susan asked.

"So you guys really like my stories," he says. "Maybe I should get into comedy."

"All you'd need is a straight man," Dave says.

Finally, she killed the scene by getting up and going to the bathroom. As she walked by us, she winked. "How's that for improvisation?" That got another laugh from everyone within earshot. When she came back, a new wench was in her chair and there was no room for her on the couches, so I jumped up and offered my place.

"Are you leaving?" Susan asked. "Please, Bruce, without the man of the hour, what will all these girls do?"

"Don't worry, I'm not leaving." I walked around and stood right behind her in back of the couch.

Keep in mind that Big Dave stayed put, so the people on the couch were still sitting with elbows touching when Joey walks up wanting to sit on Susan's lap again. Except now she says, "No way, Joey, my leg keeps falling asleep when you sit on top of me."

"Well then, make room, I'm squeezing in." When Joey forces himself between Susan and one of the other Hollywood hopefuls, Susan stretches an arm out along the backrest as if to put her arm around him, except she falls short and leaves it firmly on top. Joey even looked back, hoping it would wind up somewhere around his body. I must say I felt his pain. After all, what twenty-two-year-old hasn't played a blind fool at one time or another in his life?

Susan buried herself in conversation while Dave and I reveled in the attention we commanded. So what made me try my next move—who knows? Undoubtedly the urge to show off for the girls, but I'm afraid the lack of regard for Joey's emotions would later haunt me.

Anyway, with Susan's arm lying on the backrest and Joey dying for any kind of physical attention, I bumped the elbow of this hot number standing beside me, winked, and put my fingers on, and in, Joey's ear. Believing it was Susan, Joey seemed to twist in ecstasy as he briefly closed his eyes then reopened them halfway in a rapturous stupor. The cutie next to me could hardly contain her laughter. As this attracted the attention of our immediate crowd, she would point down to my hand with a nod of her head as I caressed Joey's blissful ear. She might as well have been saying, "Hey look, everyone, Bruce is making Joey the laughingstock of the room, and Joey doesn't even know it." Meanwhile I took great satisfaction with this humorous display as everyone laughed at Joey's expense.

Later on, after the laughter faded, Dave and I huddled up in the kitchen.

"Bruce, what's up now, how are we gonna play this?"

"I don't know, I feel guilty as hell about Joey. He wants to have a drink with us downstairs. He says he's got big news for us."

"Oh no, Bruce, please tell me we're gonna take a shot at these heart stoppers."

"Joey is the butt of all the jokes at his own party, and I'm partly responsible."

"What are you talking about, we just met the guy. Are you gonna pass on this one and only chance of a lifetime because of that little midget?"

"You can do what you want, but I think he's a classy guy, and somebody's got to tell him what a bitch his big heartthrob really is."

"Bruce, go back out in the living room and take a good look at those women you want to pass up. I mean this is like one of those unbelievable stories you read about in Playboy."

"Hey, to hell with those girls, they're probably all cokeheads anyway."

"So what, are you telling me that bothers you?"

"Hell yes, I don't know how to do that stuff. Do you? I'd probably end up sneezing it all on the floor and blowing our cover. I say we take the high road and give Joey a heads up."

"Bruce, I guarantee you, if you pass up this opportunity, you'll hate yourself for the rest of your life. And, what's worse, I'm gonna hate you the rest of your life."

"Hey, you of all people would want to know if everyone was laughing at you. And no way would you forgive me if I knew about it and didn't tell you."

"But he's not gonna buy it, and he'll probably hate you for telling him."

"Yeah, I know. Here he comes."

Joey swaggers in and ushers us towards the door. "Okay, guys, let's head down to the lounge. You can catch up with the girls later. You won't believe what's happened tonight. Oh and by the way, how about that Susan? I told you she loved me."

"Yeah, well, Dave has something to tell you about her."

"I hope it can wait, I need a drink."

A few minutes later in the lounge, I started things off again. "So, Joey, Dave wanted to tell you a few things about your girlfriend."

"Wasn't that something the way she fondled me on the couch? Couldn't keep her hands off me."

"Well, yeah, Bruce wanted to tell you about that."

"While you two are deciding who's going to tell me what, let me tell you what happened to me tonight. You guys notice the baldheaded little person with the white shoes?"

"Course we did," Dave said. "How do you miss a bald midget in out-of-style white shoes?"

Joey shot Dave a look. "Hey, we prefer to be called little people. But anyway, he calls me over and tells me he wants to talk to me privately. Then he gives me his card and tells me he owns this improvisational troupe that works out of Chicago and Ontario and would I be interested in doing some improvisation work with the troupe."

Now, color us flabbergasted. All I could say was, "Really?"

"Yeah, really, I tried to tell him that I represented Susan, but he told me to forget her, that he thought she was mocking me during the course of the night. Did you guys ever notice her mocking me?"

"Oh no, no mocking. Dave, did you notice any mocking."

"Hell no, there wasn't any mocking going on at all."

"I didn't think so, but he insisted that good-looking girls were easily replaced, but talent was hard to come by and he loved my stories and the way I delivered them."

"Can you leave Hollywood?"

"Damn right. Listen, in Hollywood, we're all just a bunch of ornaments. We never get to act. They can and do interchange us like fish. With this troupe I'll be acting, showing people what I can do. I spent years going to acting classes and all I ever get is the same kind of bit parts whenever they need a freak. Well, I'm not a freak. I'm a talented actor and now I get to prove it."

So now I have to ask, "What about Susan?"

31

Bruce McGimsey

Joey looks me square in the face and with a little twinkle in his eye he says, "Hey, it won't be the first heart I've ever broken."

He laughed and we laughed louder. "Atta boy, Joey."

Ice Cream, Cops, Greeks, and Hookers

As my first adult job, I managed a casino liquor store on the Las Vegas Strip. My boss owned a couple of casino liquor stores and a freestanding liquor store at the end of the Strip heading toward California. Since I was a young kid, fresh out of college, liquor store management hardly fulfilled an aspiring millionaire's dream, but I figured it might be the steppingstone to greater endeavors.

Simply put, I wanted a business to make some money. The fact that I knew nothing about business and had no capital meant nada. I graduated with a B-minus average from Weber State University, which had the lowest accreditation rating in the country. But no sense in belittling the only school that accepted me. Academics aside, I graduated, and being knee-deep in ambition and dreams, I needed to make my mark. Step aside, Vegas, here I come!

As I toiled away in this liquor store, two fascinating facts seemed undeniable. The liquor prices were marked up way too high, and it never appeared to matter. The tourists paid whatever the price simply out of convenience. They knew what liquor cost and it made no difference, which earned my boss a small fortune. So, I reasoned, just find a product that these suckers wanted that nobody else offered on the Strip, and I'll make a lot of jack too.

With my astute observation skills, I came up with ice cream. Granted, I knew nothing about ice cream or opening a business. Consequently, I knew nothing about health

Bruce McGimsey

department rules and restrictions or how to go about financing a startup business. Plus my nest egg totaled only about four thousand dollars.

Reasonable people, meaning my family and all my friends, predicted I'd have no chance of succeeding. No problem, what did they know? So one day my boss, the liquor store tycoon, suggested I take a look at one of the three empty units behind his liquor store at the end of the Strip. I had visited this store dozens of times and never knew these spaces existed. Well, they not only existed, they sat empty and looked perfect.

The only weakness was no one saw these units from the street. So to compensate for this problem, the landlord built a billboard at eye level between the liquor store sign and a very successful Italian restaurant adjacent to these units. The billboard, with a neon arrow underneath, was to be used exclusively to advertise the hidden units.

Enter Victor the Greek. Victor envisioned a Greek restaurant in two of the spaces. So, after these spots sat empty for almost 6 years, the landlord signed up two suckers the same week.

The rub with Victor played out like this. We needed to share the billboard sign fifty-fifty. The signs were supposed to be painted side by side with a border down the middle. Instead, Victor took the top half of the billboard without bothering to paint a border to separate our signs. In essence, Victor gave me the standard one-finger salute. For advertisement, this left me with a neon ice cream parlor sign underneath the liquor store sign, which made people think the ice cream parlor sat inside the liquor store. Who orders ice cream with Jack Daniels? So I cooked up a few four-by-eight plywood signs and conveniently arranged them to direct people to my location. As incompetent as it sounds, these makeshift mini-billboards helped a little.

I really wanted that billboard. I also needed a thousand dollars to pay a sign painter. But most of all I needed Victor and all his Greek buddies to quit gloating about how all my business came from streetwalkers.

What I didn't need was Bobby, the weasel cop. Just as business slowly improved, in walked Bobby. He showed

34

up every day for a week, about noon, and engaged me in conversation about business. Noon happened to be the only hour I got any business, but I possessed too much pride to tell him that. Nope, I led him to believe the place overflowed with business all day long.

After about a week's worth of Bobby the weasel's patronage, he asked me, "Are you aware of the fact that your signs are illegal? They're eye level and not permanently attached. You need special permits for those signs." Bobby implied that multi-million dollar hotel casinos got special permission, but that little crackerjack ice cream parlors never carried that kind of weight.

"Look," he said, "my only option is to write you citations for both signs, and then I'll be forced to remove the signs in three days. Or maybe, just maybe, we could work out a solution between the two of us." That solution of course amounted to putting fifty dollars a week, for each sign, in his pocket. Collections happened every Sunday. As long as I paid, I would never see him again.

I pleaded with him over his figures because my only alternative would be to close. Of course he said, "Between your bragging and what I've seen with my own eyes, this ice cream parlor could afford twice that much." He felt no need to budge. First, I got citations, and three days later he removed the signs just like he said.

Okay, I've got Victor the big shot taking advantage of my lack of business acumen and at the same time I've got Bobby the weasel trying to extort me out of a hundred a week. On top of all this, my best customer, Mike the drunken hobo, solicited me daily to paint my billboard sign. This bum made me crazy with his constant harassment about the sign, but since I needed business, I swallowed my last ounce of pride and allowed his harassment.

Enter Sonny, a streetwalker but by no means typical.

Sonny was a gorgeous Puerto Rican girl from New York with an engaging personality and always in a good mood. Sonny turned dewdrops into rainbows. She liked to laugh and have fun, and she loved people.

Sonny came walking into the store one day about ten in

Bruce McGimsey

the morning, which seemed way too early for her. At first I figured somebody beat her up. With one of her heels broken off and the armpits of her dress stained with sweat, the girl looked bedraggled. I poured her a large soda and inquired about her night and what had happened.

As it turned out, the blame belonged to the police, who had embarked on a new unwritten policy to rid the city of streetwalkers.

At that time, to arrest hookers they needed to record the girls soliciting a sex act for money. The police lacked the manpower and the time for this kind of endeavor. They might bust a girl or two, but not seasoned veterans. More often than not, the girls sniffed out a cop before any transactions transpired. Believing that twenty to thirty percent of crime—meaning robberies, muggings, drug trafficking, etc.—stemmed directly from prostitution, the police decided to circumvent the law. They reasoned, get the girls off the streets and out of town, and those numbers go down considerably.

Their plan of attack was to roll out a huge police bus about every two weeks and cruise down the Strip picking up Sonny plus every other hooker they found. They didn't take them to the station and book them for anything. Instead, they drove them thirty miles out the California freeway, turned right down a dusty, rock-embedded road to nowhere, and dropped these girls off behind a mountain. At this point, the police informed them they were not welcome in Las Vegas and to expect continued harassment until they left for good.

The police knew that once the girls reached the highway they could easily hitch a ride back to town, so they took them ten miles down the dirt road, where it would take hours to walk back to the highway. The girls hated taking their shoes off because of tender feet, but walking this road in heels took twice as long, not to mention the stress.

Sonny said, "Hey, a hazard of the job. I'm not going to leave, the money's too good."

Although the cops constantly picked them up for vagrancy or loitering, Sonny felt the never-ending infringement of their rights would stop. But after I told her about my run-in with Bobby the weasel, we concluded that cops never relented,

36

and persevere as we might, we both figured to capitulate in the end.

Two weeks went by after my conversation with Sonny. Meanwhile, my ice cream venture crumbled before my eyes. I felt clueless. With no money and no business, my options seemed limited. Then, one night as I headed home, about halfway down the Strip I saw a huge white bus and a cop car pulled over in front of it. Sure enough, at least twenty girls sat in the bus while two cops escorted five more girls up the ramp.

With nothing better to do, I pulled over down the road a ways and watched the action. Just like Sonny said, the bus continued down the Strip while the police methodically went about their quest, picking up every hooker in sight. The Strip started at the Sahara Hotel, and in those days, ended at the Tropicana, so as you drove Las Vegas Boulevard, you eventually hooked up with the California highway. An hour later, when they reached the end of the Strip, they had stuffed fifty to sixty girls onto that bus.

I followed this paddy wagon straight out the California highway, and true to form, about thirty miles out, it turned right onto a road that apparently had never been named. I kept driving straight down the highway to a rest stop half a mile up the divide so I could follow the bus's taillights and watch it disappear around a mountain range. Thirty to forty minutes later, a pair of headlights appeared on the same road and made its way back. The bus got to the highway, cut across the median, and turned left, back toward Vegas and the police motor pool.

With no real plan, I headed out this road hoping to find Sonny amongst this troop, figuring to give her a ride back to the city. I switched off my headlights just in case a highway patrolman lurked about. I drove at least ten miles before I got to the girls. They walked mostly in small groups, and as I drove past them, they ran up yelling, "Give me a ride, honey. Hey, honey, I'll make it worth your while." But I didn't see Sonny. Finally, about fifty yards past the last girl, Sonny's voice rang out. I pulled over, and while most of the girls trotted toward my car, Sonny raced to it.

Panting, Sonny said to me, "Bruce, they'll pay you big money for a ride back to town. Let me handle it." Sonny took over.

What a power trip. I had at least fifty young, mostly beautiful women begging. It took about two minutes before the bickering started. Sonny had them bidding for a spot in my car, which happened to be a little Ford Pinto. I'm thinking, legally, I could fit a girl in my front bucket seat, three in the back seat, and get away with one sitting uncomfortably on the console between the driver and passenger.

Thank heaven for Sonny, who thought bigger. Besides those five passengers who got passage back to town, she knew the girls really just needed a ride to the main highway, where they could hitchhike. Since nobody ever saw another car on this road, if we ran into one, it undoubtedly meant the police, which also meant I'm screwed anyway. So Sonny reasoned, why not gamble? For $100 apiece, five of the girls got a ride into town. For $50 apiece, she put a girl on her lap and another standing up with a leg on each bucket seat and her head sticking up through my sunroof. She put two extra girls in the back seat on laps. With the trunk open, she sat two girls with their legs hanging out the back, and one more girl on the hood in the front of the passenger's seat with her legs dangling down the side of the car. Sonny wanted a free ticket and the power to pick and choose who got a ride back.

To the girls, this equaled highway robbery. But Sonny knew they'd pay it. With all the competition stuck out in the desert, the girls who made it back that night had a corner on the market or shall we say at least a corner all to themselves. Of course, lots of girls made me offers to the tune of "I'll take care of you for a free ride." But as a young entrepreneur in dire need of money, I figured why barter when I held the upper hand?

I had no thought of the wear on my car putting all that weight on it. I saw dollar signs. I made a point to drive extra slowly with all the girls hanging off my car. Since this was a consistent occurrence every two or three weeks, later on I started borrowing my father's truck, never once comprehending that if I got caught, my father's truck would be impounded. The phrase "hauling ass" became my slogan.

So what would happen if the cops caught me? Who knew? When you're young and stupid, you feel bulletproof. I did know that my new shuttle business allowed me the capital to pay a sign painter for my half of the billboard, which brings me back to Mike, the hobo.

Somewhere in between the time Victor commandeered the top half of the billboard sign and Sonny and I started the streetwalker transportation system, Mike the hobo began frequenting my establishment. I asked the liquor store manager about this vagrant, and all he knew was that Mike bought a pint of cheap vodka five times a week. Mike supposedly drove a taxi, even though I never saw it. He claimed he parked it on the other side of the Italian restaurant, where he needed to come in a couple of times a week to fulfill a business obligation with the owner. The restaurant owner, rumored to be a loan shark, explained why Mike hung around. In Las Vegas, the way cops hassled cab drivers, this figured to be big trouble for Mike, unless of course he lied about driving a taxi. Since I never believed he really drove a taxi, I never believed he painted signs either, but he still constantly hit me up to paint my billboard.

I lacked respect for Mike, figuring him for a delusional drunk. Apparently, cab companies never bothered with dress codes. Anyway, when I pulled up one morning and found Mike up on his ladder with painters' chalk in hand, I exploded. The simple truth was that I didn't have the fiber to stop him. I envisioned Victor and his cronies laughing hysterically at my sign. Somehow, Mike got the impression that I'd given him the okay to paint my sign. Somebody here lived in fantasyland.

That sign equaled my last shot at making my business go. So when I told Mike what I wanted on the sign, he said, "Relax, leave everything to me. You're going to love it." I sighed, rolled my eyes in disgust, and walked away, sensing Victor's laughter.

First, Mike drew a banana split and "Ice Cream Parlor" freehand. He used the painting chalk but didn't bother with a measuring device to make his letters straight or correctly spaced. What idiot would let a bum off the street paint the sign that held the future to his success? Because my business traffic seemed to crawl, all I could do was stew over my poor judgment. Or should I say lack of spine?

Every two minutes I walked out expecting to see a nightmare unfolding, and instead I kept walking back in thinking, not bad. Until finally I started thinking this guy cooks. The lettering was even and the banana split looked like a creamery delight.

Make no mistake, Mike deserved artist stature. I likened the sign painters I solicited to wannabe artists, while on the other hand, Mike was an artist forced to be a sign painter. Later, I learned that he had worked for a Pennsylvania dairy for a number of years painting banana splits, strawberry sundaes, milkshakes, etc., on billboards. He did the lettering, the colors, the creativity, everything. So this banana split cut right in his wheelhouse. No doubt Mike put in his time in the art world. He never hit the big time with his art, but still worked at it and sold a painting from time to time.

For the rest of the day, I watched Mike with awe and fascination as he perfected his lettering. Also, the banana split he drew got better and better as he filled in each luscious scoop of ice cream and added the toppings, nuts, and cherry. He owned an old station wagon full of ladders and various paints, which he used to finalize his masterpiece. But the real brilliance still needed to be displayed.

Victor named the Greek restaurant Plaka. I think plaka meant restaurant in Greek. So Victor's sign simply read, in big, blue lettering, "Plaka." Surrounding the lettering were small separate paintings of various fruits, grapes, bananas, etc. The lettering appeared to be in some kind of Greek style, I guess to remind people of Greece.

Mike matched my background paint with Victor's. Instead of painting "K.C. Ann's Ice Cream Parlor," my shop's name, he just painted "Ice Cream Parlor." Plus, he made the ice cream parlor lettering in the same Greek style as Victor's Plaka lettering, and the same color. Thus, the billboard read seemed to read "Plaka Ice Cream Parlor."

The fruit on Victor's half of the sign just happened to fit in with my ice cream parlor concept. Mike, the genius, had managed to steal Victor's half of the sign. Instead of my part of the sign being just the bottom half, it now looked like the whole thing advertised my business alone.

I guessed that maybe one in one hundred knew what Plaka meant. Once in a while, people asked me if I sold Greek food. Or sometimes I got, "Hey, buddy, that's kind of an odd name for an ice cream parlor." But mostly I got, "Hey, we'll take three banana splits, just like that painting outside."

The first night, a couple of hours after Mike finished the sign, business had already improved dramatically. Soon I needed help to wait on customers, so I finally started making money from the sweat of my employee's brow, and I laughed at myself for putting Mike beneath me. I needed to learn that I had a lot to learn.

About a year and a half later, I ended up selling the business for a nice profit. Of course I reasoned that I would parlay that money into something really huge. I didn't take into account how lucky I got having both Sonny and Mike enter my life with such perfect timing. I never fully appreciated the break that the police didn't discover my circumvention of their streetwalker policy, which could have gotten real ugly. No, I figured myself for a date with the big time and this sufficed as just an introduction.

As for Victor, while he and his friends walked to his car checking out the parlor's ample business, I rushed to the door and pointed to the sign. "Hey Victor, nice sign you put together. I bet it really packs the joint." I gave him a thumbs-up. Then I smiled, he shook his head, and his friends laughed. Life was sweet after all.

Crap Tables 101

"No roll, one die slipped out of hand."

"What are you talking about? Both dice are on the table and the stick man called twelve. That's a craps roll. Now pay up."

Hell, is this what I'd gone through eight weeks of craps school for? Then worked three different craps dealing jobs in one year? Just to acquire the skills to obtain a job here?

I had been dealing dice or craps at one of the more elite downtown joints in Las Vegas. It wasn't the money you'd make at a Strip casino, but it was more than the standard ten and fifteen bucks I made at the lowlife grind joints I previously worked. Four more years of this and I would accrue the skills I needed to get a real job out on the Strip. That's where the big money was. But for now, I had to deal with this.

This casino allowed twenty-five-cent minimum crap bets and maxed out at five-hundred-dollar bets. At most of the downtown houses, twenty-five-cent crap bets meant all low-level players. Not so at my current job. They got low-level action along with multimillionaires.

Now, the hardest thing in dealing craps was that as soon as the dice hit a number, every player at the table started chattering, instructing you as to what they wanted done with their bets—same bet, press it, take it down with odds, etc. So you try to tune everyone out except for your first payout. At the same time, you listened for your box man, any of the floor men, or any of the pit bosses, in case you made a wrong payout, which happened constantly.

Generally, in a break-in house, you looked to get out of there as soon as you got enough experience to be hired elsewhere. As for the few downtown joints that looked for and handled the same type of big-time action as the Strip casinos, they needed legitimate dealers, not beginners. The problem for us dealers was that handling bigger action downtown didn't mean you made Strip-type tips. The best downtown house I worked in, one of the classiest, only fetched fifty to sixty dollars in tips a day.

Thus, even the classy downtown casinos couldn't attract legitimate dealers. What they got were guys who were better than break-ins, but not seasoned dealers, at least not yet. Meaning me. The relevance of all this was that if you looked to cheat a casino, specifically at dice, you wanted to find a casino that sweated the money when they started to lose.

One afternoon, we had a real steamer brewing. The game was as hot as it could get, at least for a rookie dealer like me. People threw bets in from three rows deep. You played hell keeping track of everyone and where they all stood, but worse than that, we were losing. Understand, when one of the downtown casinos lost big time, management theorized that the dealers needed to move the dice faster. The game's odds laid out in the house's favor. Therefore, the more rolls thrown, the better the house's chance of taking advantage of its built-in edge. The big disadvantage, the faster the dice moved, the more pressure it put on the hacks dealing the game. Obviously, mistakes would be made, and worse yet, certain types looked to capitalize on those mistakes.

Your stick man, me, controlled the game, passed the dice to the proper shooter, took in all proposition bets, which are the long-shot bets in the middle of the table (hard six, hard eight, eleven, any craps, etc.) When the dice hit, the stick man called the number the dice landed on. He also took responsibility for the side of the table the dice rolled to. He retrieved the dice and then watched that side of the table to make sure the dealer made his payouts properly. He then collected the losing proposition bets and saw that winning proposition bets were paid out. You also had two other dealers on both ends of the table who placed and booked the players' bets. Then when the dice landed, they scooped up the losers first, and paid out the winners.

In this particular game, all the players knew the intricacies of craps. Meaning, when the dice hit, most of the players were paid to the max because they were taking advantage of the better odds allowed for certain types of bets. But there were three people, two middle-aged men and a younger woman, playing the field. The field, a large box on both sides and in the front half of the table, was reachable by the players, who didn't have to rely on dealers to place bets for them but placed their own. The field consisted of the numbers two, three, four, nine, ten, eleven, and twelve. These were one-time bets won or lost on each roll of the dice.

Field bets are sucker bets. The house has the best of the odds, so if you make field roll bets long enough, the house will get your money. Anyway, the two men and one woman were standing together making five-dollar field bets every roll.

Now, the woman held the dice and rolled winning numbers for three or four minutes. The stick man, me, pushed the dice back to the lady while at the same time still taking proposition bets from her two gentlemen friends. By rights, I should have pulled the dice from the lady roller until all the proposition bets were placed. But I didn't. I kept taking bets until the lady rolled the dice again. Since, under these circumstances, the bosses always pressured the stick man to move the dice quicker to keep the game moving, it allowed the threesome to make their move.

Another of the stick man's jobs was to follow the dice and make sure they both hit the end of the table. If, for whatever reason, the dice didn't reach the end of the table, the stick man called off the bet, yelling out, "No roll!" And he needed to do it before the dice quit moving. If a die slipped out of a player's hand, or did not hit the end of the table, or landed on someone's bet, or flew off the table, the stick man had to call off the bet. If not, it's a bet, and the players needed to be paid.

So now, the lady held the dice and her two friends occupied my attention with prop bets. While I reached for a misdirected chip, the lady and her two friends pushed three five-hundred-dollar bets into the field, the maximum bet allowed. At the same time, with the dice already in her hand, she set one die down in front of her on the number six and in the same motion, she rolled the other die to the end of the table. What I as the stick man or, for that matter, either one of the other two dealers should have done was scream out, "No roll!" while the second die was still in the air. Unfortunately, that didn't happen.

The lady cheated. By setting one die down on the number six, she increased her and her two friends' odds of winning to better than eighty percent. Remember, the field roll numbers are two, three, four, nine, ten, eleven, and twelve. So all they needed to win was for the second die not to land on one or two. Any other number and the three of them win. The other die landed on six, making the roll twelve, known as boxcars, paying triple. So the three cheaters didn't just win five hundred, they each won fifteen hundred dollars. Needless to say, this might make a casino angry.

The casino manager exploded. He was upset with us and was particularly mad at the three players. The cheaters who pulled this off tried to leave the table. But the unwritten rules stated that the shooter kept the dice until they seven out. The woman was having a good roll, and the rest of the players were winning money, so instead of getting out of Dodge with the ill-gotten cash, the woman finished out the roll. This gave the casino time to plot its next move.

Next thing you know, security surrounded the two gentlemen. They told the woman to go cash in all of her chips and pull her car up to the side entrance. Her two friends were needed briefly in the casino manager's office.

Thirty minutes later, security rolled the two guys out in wheelchairs. They handed these guys a beating of a lifetime, then paraded them through the casino so everyone could witness it. The casino wanted people to ask questions and spread the word. If you're going to take your shot, bad things will happen. I never heard about any repercussions, lawsuits, etc. Thirty-five years ago, the town ran a little differently.

My day got worse. Five minutes after the cheaters got theirs, a new dealer showed up, tapped me out for break, and two security guards escorted me to the casino manager's office.

In the office, three of the largest, most well built knuckle crunchers, all wearing security uniforms, greeted me with the sternest of looks. The casino manager offered me a chair. When I refused, he told me it would be in my best interest to sit.

Right about now I'd like to tell you that I conjured up some clever banter and threatened to unleash my massive left hook if any fisticuffs ensued. But the truth was, I never felt so afraid. He wanted to know if I colluded with the cheaters because my stick play got so sloppy at such a key time. I assured him over and over of my innocence and finally walked out of that office untouched with my job intact. This shook me to the point of deciding I needed a career change, and eventually, I made that change. I'll never know for sure how close I came, but I figured, who needs this?

Fifteen years later, I would be knee-deep in the food and beverage end of the casino business dealing with our biggest problem, the culinary union. They would hassle and harass management constantly. So one night, while I'm negotiating with my casino's union rep about a grievance she wanted to file, she told me that they never filed a grievance against the downtown casino I had dealt craps for fifteen years earlier. Most hotels, the union filed as many as three hundred grievances a year. But with that particular casino, they always gave it a pass. She said they just did not care to make that casino mad.

Crazy Debbie

Without a doubt, Crazy Debbie ranks as the strangest girl I had ever met. One spring afternoon, when the population of Vegas ranged about eighty thousand people (certainly not a hick town), a friend and I drove down a back street. We never expected to see this voluptuous brunette strutting down the sidewalk, shaking and shimmying. We both laughed aloud because her miniskirt cut so high that with every left step she took, half her ham flashed.

My first thought, of course, she must be a working girl forced into walking home from a deal gone sour. Well, if you're a guy who fancies himself a world-class detective, with nothing to do on a late spring afternoon, you investigate. Excuse the pun, but I wanted to get to the bottom of this. Being a trooper, I hung a U-turn, pulled up beside her, and began the interrogation. My friend Larry rode shotgun and appeared just as intrigued. Without hesitation, she walked up to the window and leaned in. "What's doing in this boring town?"

Her low-cut blouse, featuring that forever-stylish no-bra look, showed us just how ample a real woman could be. If this girl wasn't a hooker, she sure missed a good bet. Me, being totally stunned and a bit preoccupied with her physical attributes, mustered only the very basic of lines. "Hey, we're going down to the Brewery to pound a few. You in?"

She opened my door. "Debbie. I've been in town a week. I'm bored, I'm thirsty, and I really feel like dancing."

At the time, I guessed her for a stripper with no regard for modesty. She jumped into our car and immediately started

49

complimenting us on our looks and build. She made up excuses to touch us on the knee or shoulder, just like a vintage stripper trying to entice you into a lap dance. Adamant about going dancing, I no longer figured her for a hooker. Hmm, let's just see where this night takes us.

When we got to the Brewery, a place I frequented a lot, I received all sorts of shrill catcalls and hand slaps. The only person I knew was Lynn, the barmaid. Yet the clientele, mostly guys, insisted on shaking hands and giving me the thumbs up sign. What's going on here? Per Lynn, it turned out Debbie had visited the bar a couple of nights earlier. Lynn told me Debbie had gotten drunk and taken a young man upstairs to a loft the tavern used only on weekends. The place featured a nice secluded area where a couple could do things and still maintain some privacy. The buzz around the tavern suggested that the two of them succumbed to carnal desires up there. So I asked Lynn, "Were you an eyewitness to this debauchery?"

"No. But the lucky guy bragged about his conquest and basked in his own bravado for the rest of the night." So if she was a professional, she sure wasn't very good at it.

One beer, and Debbie wanted to dance. In those days, dancing meant going to the Hermitage, a county rock bar thirty miles or so up a narrow winding road through a dangerous canyon that offered a single lane with steep valleys. Not the best place to drive after drinking a few. However, being sober now, we piled into the car and started on down the road for some good old-fashioned two-stepping.

Larry bowed out of the action to give me a clean shot at raising my embarrassingly low batting average. Debbie appeared to be the perfect answer. Talkative, fun, extremely extroverted on the dance floor, she did whatever it took to keep every eyeball glued to her. All eyes needed to focus on her. If she caught a guy not watching her, she jumped between that guy and his partner, danced as provocatively as she could, and eventually rubbed up against the guy. If you can, picture a hundred infuriated women and about a hundred and fifty turned-on guys. Except now, every man in the joint thought he deserved a shot at my date. I daresay most of them took that shot.

To me, girls who craved that kind of attention spelled big trouble, but for one night, I overlooked strange. By now, my head swirled with wild fantasies of things to come regardless of her peculiarities. As a true focused detective, I wanted to accomplish a number of tasks. I needed to kill another hour at the tavern, not get too drunk to drive, fend off all the circling sharks, get her back to my house, and show her a small slice of heaven.

Go time finally arrived. Debbie's body looked like something to the tune of an Anna Nicole or Jayne Mansfield, not fat, but she really couldn't afford five more pounds. Indifferent to any parts of her body that might be exposed, she seemed to have a help-yourself policy. What I mean by that, she seemed to feature, shall I say, an easygoing virtue. At this point, I hoped to channel all of my energy onto the treacherous drive through a steep, narrow canyon just to get back home. Now that I was behind the wheel, I wished I'd left my last beer full. So here I sat, as distracted as any typical lustful man would be, trying like crazy to concentrate, while this heavenly tart shamelessly flaunted her body. Suddenly, Crazy Debbie hauled off and smacked me across the back of my head. Then she followed that up with three more punches to my face and chest. Fortunately, barely maintaining my concentration throughout the thrashing, I managed to stay on the narrow road instead of plunging us down the canyon.

Crazy Debbie stood a good five foot seven, weighed at least a hundred forty pounds, and packed one mean wallop. Besides that, she wore a ring that protruded from her middle finger like a brass knuckle. So I pulled over onto the side of the road, not just angry but flustered. My first instinct was to dump her out and make her walk. The trouble with that plan, half the town saw me with her. What if she ended up dead? No, even though dreams of sexual interludes appeared all but shattered, I figured to get her home and be done with her. Not to say she hadn't earned a piece of my mind.

After a few of my choicest comments, usually reserved only for bitter enemies, I asked her what her problem was. She sheepishly looked at me and shrugged her shoulders. I

Bruce McGimsey

asked her again and still got the same response. What could I do? I started the car and headed down the road, boiling over, furious, and thinking just get this nut to her door.

Now that I had both hands on the steering wheel and was locked in deep concentration, Debbie started talking to me in a French accent and calling herself Arlette. "Ooh, I'm so sorrey. Did Arlette hurt you? Let me keese it and make it better." Then she started kissing me on the cheek, approximately the same area where she smacked me a few times moments earlier. Next, she took my arm and put it around her shoulder. I suppose to an average person this would seem very strange. But, understand: on my fantasy meter, the needle already hit the super hot zone, that delusional euphoria a man gets when anticipating a sexual encounter. It took me all of about two minutes to forget the welt her ring plastered on my face, and I continued where I left off.

No sooner did I reach the outskirts of town than the crazy wench started belting me again. This bitch tuned me up for the second time and I'm not talking love taps, I'm talking haymakers. I drove with my left hand while defending my life with my right. The knots on my head from that damn ring swelled up like berries, so I pulled over and started screaming at her. I was just short of hitting her back. Talk about battered and abused, along about now I felt like a borrowed mule at sundown. So I started the car back up, asked her directions to her place, and beat a steady course for exactly where she told me to go.

She took me down a dirt road just off Main Street. I thought I knew every nook and hole in this town, but she directed me to these obscure little one-room huts about ten yards by ten yards, maybe a row of seven or eight of them. Here I sat with the strangest woman I'd ever met, in front of these little shacks. I'm thinking, no need to be subtle.

"Get out, bitch. And don't look back."

Do you really think that's what happened? Not a chance! She refused to get out of my car. Instead, she started the French girl routine again. Now, of course, a little tiny part of my brain told me, don't be a sucker for this act again. But a great big huge mass of my brain said, man, she looks good!

52

This time, without being too graphic, she put her hands all over me while feeding me all those same lines and turning all the right dials.

What can I say? Deep down I kind of expected her to start the fisticuffs again. So when she did, I deflected most of her punches. Only this time my patience wore thin. I told her to get out, and I got a little physical with her. I didn't hit her, but I manhandled her trying to wrestle her out of my car. So now this loony tune, instead of going quietly, hung on for dear life. Whenever she saw an opening, she threw more fists, with an occasional kick. The tougher I got, the rougher she got.

Just when I thought I'd finally out-muscled her, she whispered to me, "Yeah, that's what I'm looking for."

Holy hell, I've run smack dab into a Sybil clone! How many different personalities did Sybil have? How many personalities had Crazy Debbie already shown me? Come on, brain, think. Didn't Sybil have a serial killer as one of her alter egos? Wow! Get a load of this body! Am I really going to turn this body loose? Of course I am. If I walk into that room, she will kill me, and take great pleasure in it. Nope, I said to myself, get this wacko out of your car. And quit looking at her body, you idiot.

Crazy Debbie licked her lips and shimmied her shoulders, creating a ripple effect that worked its way down her chest and back up again. "I've got the whole setup in my room. You're going to love it."

"Bitch, get the hell out of my car."

Suddenly, the top half of her dress came down.

"Hey, that's great," I said, "but I ain't in the mood." I kept telling myself, don't be stupid, it's not worth the risk...but wait a minute, hold it, somewhere in Sybil's background, wasn't one of those thirteen personalities a nymphomaniac? Or could I be over-thinking things here?

Probably now would be the perfect time to give you my friend Larry's classic definition of a horndog. A horndog is an idiot, usually male, who will risk life, limb, and all semblance of pride for a one-in-a-billion chance of a sexual encounter.

This time, instead of my dragging her out of the car, we

just stepped out and walked right through the door. What can I say? One-in-a-billion were better odds than most of my nights.

It didn't take five minutes before she took off her clothes and slipped into this outrageous leather outfit. Just as she'd promised, the room all but overflowed with S & M paraphernalia. She handed me a leather mask and told me to take off my shirt. She insisted I play a seventeenth-century jailer with a heavy English brogue.

I felt like I'd walked into the set of a cheap, sadistic porn movie. Come to think of it, maybe that was what happened. I remember thinking that before I left, I'd better check for cameras. For me, this amounted to nothing except laughs and giggles. But I knew she meant business, especially when she handed me a cat-of-nine tails and, in a French accent, told me to whip her until I saw welts. Now, I can't do an English accent, and just forget about whipping her, but most of all, by now there was no chance of even keeping a straight face.

As events unfolded, and unbeknownst to me, the police cruised by her place every forty-five minutes. When they pulled up in front of her hut, you just couldn't miss that distinct police radio or that unmistakable red flashing illumination through the cracks of her heavily covered window. Yup, it's the cops. What kind of kinky, perverse sex crime waited for me on my upcoming rap sheet? I pictured them making me hold up the mask as they booked and photographed me.

Right off, Crazy Debbie told me, "Don't worry about it. Just tell them I'm your girlfriend. This isn't against the law." So what did this sicko do next? She opened the door and invited them in, not at all embarrassed by her outfit. Worst of all, she stayed in character and maintained her French accent. At least I managed to put my shirt back on.

Now I'm here to tell you, the cops enjoyed giving me the needle with all their sarcastic remarks. In their shoes, I'd have laughed too. Now Crazy Debbie says, "He's my boyfriend and we didn't do anything illegal. We broke no laws. Tell them, um…" Right then it became painfully obvious that she forgot my name. The head cop looked at me with a smirk to verify her story. Okay, here was my chance to be her hero and show her that these cops didn't intimidate me.

"Fat chance," I said to the cops. "I don't know her from Adam, and for sure I don't know or care about her troubles. I certainly want no part of jail."

So, Crazy Debbie cussed at me like a New Yorker in a traffic jam. I looked at her, shrugged my shoulders, and in my best French accent said, "I'm so sor-rey. Did Brucie make you ang-reeey?"

After this night, I swore I'd never again serve as an example of Larry's horndog definition.

Thank God
for Archie Bunker

Every once in a while, even the shallowest of men will take a reflective look at himself. On one of my soul-searching inward moments, I concluded I needed to settle down. Now, the only girl I had ever loved, Gineel, had already dumped me twice. But since it had been over a year since our last encounter, I reasoned, "Hey, this girl has suffered enough." So I temporarily moved back to Utah to give this woman one more shot at the title.

This time things went pretty well. In two weeks, I landed a job. Gineel completely succumbed to my ever-abundant charms. Also, I hooked up with a couple of my old pool-playing buddies from college. Besides their excellent nine-ball skills, they were honed in on some of the best no-limit poker games in the area.

So in two snaps I had a loving girlfriend, a good job, and best of all, I made bank on the weekends gambling. For about six months, life couldn't have been sweeter. But, in a gambler's world, there are rules. The first rule being: suckers are not suckers forever. The second rule: give a sucker a break and you're a sucker yourself. Translation, we gave up too much weight in our nine-ball games, and our fish greatly improved at the all-night poker game. The easy action dried up and we were at a loss, literally.

One weekend, Gineel left for a Colorado River boat trip. No problem, I figured to spend the weekend playing pool and poker and hopefully making some money. Our only concern was where to go to find some gambling.

Bruce McGimsey

We finally decided this might be a good time to make a run for the border—the Wyoming border. At that time, a series of mining towns skirted the Wyoming-Utah line. These boomtowns offered good jobs for unskilled laborers. Hard work equaled great money. Of course, good pool-playing skills along with smooth hustling technique also equaled great money. At least, so we thought. Our plan was to cruise the bars and weed out all the hookers, pimps, and cowboys. Then focus on the mineworkers or, shall we say, the unskilled, well-paid suckers.

So, here I was up in Wyoming with my friend Billy Byner and another friend, Big Dave. Big Dave still weighed in right at 400 pounds, and both guys played excellent pool. If you ranked them nationally, they'd be also-rans, maybe in the top 1,000 players. But in Podunk, Wyoming, they might as well have been world champions.

We started the weekend playing low-limit pool, trying to get somebody tied on. We bought drinks, let our opponents win occasionally, and at the same time kept looking out for pigeons. We figured that if we kept the drinks flowing, sooner or later pigeons hovered, and that's exactly what happened.

The three of us hooked up with a group of drunken Mexicans playing on separate tables for twenty a game. This scenario presented great possibilities.

Right here the plan went awry. Big Dave started drinking while trying to loosen up our opponents. Huge mistake! When the big guy drank, he fancied himself a clever guy. Trying to beat someone out of all of his money cuts a thin line between clever and obnoxious. As a guy's wallet thins out, he doesn't want to hear it. Especially if miraculously, his opponent's game sharpens up in the last hour as the size of the bet increases.

Next thing you know, the Mexicans tap out and are extremely angry. Now we've got drunk Mexicans and a big fat guy gloating about his winnings and making fun of them. I tried to slow up Dave's big mouth, but he found himself hilarious.

The Mexicans finally left, and I told my friends, "Let's blow. I don't like the feel of things."

"Sure," Dave said. "I've just got to hit the john and shake hands with my best friend." He didn't have a care in the

58

world. While he was in the bathroom, one of the Mexicans he embarrassed came back into the bar.

I don't speak Spanish, but puto, gringo, gordo, and donde were some of the words I remembered from high school. Normally, a little guy like this wasn't going to be a threat, but this particular little Mexican carried a gun. Now, I don't remember who originated The Wave, maybe fans at the University of Michigan created the first. Anyway, this night, I witnessed it for the first time.

As this guy surveyed the room looking for Dave the fat gringo, his gun also surveyed the room, and each time that pistol swept through the place, every head and torso went down and then back up, just like The Wave at a ballgame. It sure appeared like the Mexican meant business. Fortunately, Dave didn't come out of the bathroom, and we convinced the pequeño pistolero that he was two bars down in another pool game.

So, the angry Latino left, giving us a chance to slither out. Except, where the hell did Billy go? Dave strolls out of the bathroom wearing a broad smile until I say to him, "Your last opponent brought a gun back, and he wanted to share one of his jokes with you." Now Billy shows up at the door with fire in his eyes. No problem, let's just go.

We had parked our car in a U-shaped dirt lot with one entrance in and out. Three back doors of three different bars all had immediate access to this parking lot. About twenty yards from our car, we saw a group of four or five Mexicans standing by the back door of the bar next to ours. They didn't appear threatening and completely ignored us. Next thing I knew, Billy yelled out some typical racial slur, pulled out a gun of his own, and popped off at least three rounds before I shoved his arm up.

I screamed at him, "These aren't even the same guys!"

"The hell they aren't!"

Meanwhile, the group had scurried through the back door of the bar, shouting in Spanish, with one exception. One poor guy got shot in the heel, so now he had one leg up in his hand doing the hotfoot, dancing around like a scene from the Three Stooges.

Bruce McGimsey

We quickly hopped into Dave's car and headed out of town. About five minutes later, just before we reached the freeway, two deputy sheriffs from this small Wyoming town pulled us over. These two guys were doing a Barney and Gomer routine that could have been hilarious, except for the fact that they weren't playing around.

Guns drawn, they told us, "Throw out your weapons first and step out of the car one at a time. Now, lie down on the ground, face kissing the pavement so we can cuff you."

Right about here I'm thinking, this can't be good.

With the three of us cuffed in the backseat, the two deputies took great delight telling us what the charges would be. "Guys, it's got to be attempted murder no matter who's the shooter. We'll take you to jail and then go back and do a crime scene investigation. It will probably take us the rest of the night, and, of course, we'll have to call Judge Peterson off his duck-hunting trip. That ought to make him good and ornery."

Their excitement about our predicament nauseated me, but what could we do? I figured our best move, just be quiet. But not Big Dave.

"Hey, Barney, if it's duck season, shouldn't you and Gomer go hide in the broom closet so you don't get shot?"

"Keep it up, fat boy, and my name ain't Barney," one deputy snapped.

"Well, if you ain't Barney, what does Gomer here call you?"

"Well, fat boy, tomorrow the judge will call you a potential inmate."

Now, I don't mind admitting these two deputies had me scared to death. I didn't sleep at all that night thinking about prison. On the other hand, my two idiot friends zonked right out, not a care in the world. They figured the knucklehead deputies would screw something up.

Nine a.m. rolled up and it was time to face the judge. Sure enough, this judge seemed like he had a beehive down his pants, while both deputies eagerly barked out what they found at the crime scene.

"Judge," Gomer said, "Here's the report. We think it's attempted murder."

So the judge started thumbing through the paperwork. A

60

little agitated, he thumbed through them again. Then he glared at the deputy. "I don't see the attempted murder charge."

"It's in there, judge, honest."

The judge frowned, then rustled through the papers again. This time he read their names. "Okay, we've got Hector Garcia, Juan Dominquez, Rudy Silvera." Clearly annoyed, he slapped the papers down on his bench. "All I see here is a wetback got shot in the foot. Is that what you're talking about?" He looked at us and shook his head. "Okay, fellas, fifty-dollar fine, disturbing the peace, now get the hell out of my court."

Then he pointed at the deputies. "I'll see you two Monday morning, and if that's it, I'm going duck hunting."

With the judge out of the room and the fines paid, one last cheap shot at the numbskull twins seemed appropriate. "Oh, Barney, the judge is going to take away your bullet," mimicked Dave and Billy in unison.

Probably about now, most people would be thanking God they escaped this unfortunate event with a mere misdemeanor. I must admit that I breathed a gigantic sigh of relief as we walked out of the jailhouse. But there are things to remember. First off, our car had been impounded, and Barney saw to it that hours went by before we retrieved it, which left us back at a bar killing time.

Since we had no better place to be while we waited, why not play a little pool and maybe wager on the outcome? After all, it was still only Saturday, and maybe a few of these Wyomingites had a little money left in their pockets. Normally, I never mixed nine-ball and alcohol, but when one goes from an attempted-murder rap to a $50 misdemeanor beef, why not enjoy one celebratory toast? Besides, having graduated from Weber State University, we figured we were smarter than everyone else. Who could have guessed that one celebratory toast would lead to six more and we'd wind up winning hundreds?

So five hours later, with pockets full of money and snoots full of liquor, we secured the car from impound and hit the highway home. Have you ever heard the phrase, "Don't drink and drive"? As we drove through our first major turn, Dave rolled the car off the road and down a canyon about forty yards or so. He and I got a few bumps and scratches but our best

61

Bruce McGimsey

guess for Billy was a broken collarbone or maybe worse.

Having legal beagles in the family, I knew big trouble loomed. If somebody gets hurt because of a drunk driver, this adds up to a felony, and if this felony occurred in Barney's jurisdiction, watch out, Dave.

We needed a plan. It took about five minutes for a trucker to call what we assumed was the highway patrol. I crawled through the back window of our upside-down car, pulled out the case of beer, and buried it about seventy-five yards further down the canyon. Sure enough, I got back in time to see Barney and Goober pull up. The twinkle in Barney's eye and the joy on his face suggested this moment was one of the happiest of Barney's life. I also knew this because Barney told us so in those exact words.

When Barney quit laughing, he asked, "Guys, who was driving?"

"Barney," Dave arrogantly said, "I honestly don't know, I was asleep in the back."

"Barney, don't look at me, I was sleeping in the back seat too."

"So you were driving," Barney says to Billy, who was holding his arm and looked like he was about to puke from the pain.

"Oh no, I was sleeping in the back seat."

"Hey, somebody was driving. I'll bust all three of you for this and you'll all get popped for a felony. You guys are going to outsmart yourself this time."

"Sure, Barney."

"Okay, fat boy, wait till we put you in the box back at the station. I promise you, we'll find out in a Minnesota minute just who caused this accident."

Goober gave all three of us sobriety tests and none of us passed, but they had to airlift Billy to a hospital, which left Dave and me to face Barney's wrath. All of this took about an hour before we headed back to man-up to the blistering browbeating that the knucklehead twins were about to administer.

Still, they couldn't prove who drove as long as we didn't cop to it, and we knew it, so Dave never quit baiting Barney. I must admit the two of them got to be laughable. One time Barney

62

interrupted my interrogation to tell me that Dave rolled on me and I had two minutes to own up to the truth or he would take Dave's story to the judge.

"Barney," I said, "don't you think I watch television?"

They even tried switching interrogators and sent the female dispatcher in to grill me, figuring I'd wilt under a woman's charms.

Finally, about midnight, Barney stormed out of Dave's room to answer the phone. From Barney's whining, we figured it to be the judge. Barney hung up and stomped into my room. "Get your fat friend, leave, and don't ever come back to my town again." Then he walked away, presumably to avoid seeing us gloat.

Here we were at midnight, our car totaled, with no way to get home until the nine a.m. bus. Two Weber State graduates with pockets full of money. Do you think we headed to a motel, or back to a bar for a little nine-ball? Take a wild guess.

I got back to my apartment just as Gineel pulled up, back from her boat trip. I helped her up the stairs with her weekend bag.

"Did you do anything exciting this weekend, Bruce?"

I gave Gineel an extra-tight hug. "Nope, nothing much."

Now, I like to think that I'm not prejudiced or bigoted. After all, my grandmother was Mexican. But I've got to tell you. When I think of the direction my life could have taken, old Judge Peterson will always own a little corner of my heart.

I'm Having a Good Day

Here is a little-known fact that should be categorized in your gee-whiz file—the gee-whiz file being that section of your brain which stores useless information. During the Mafia's heyday in Las Vegas, the period from the fifties through the late seventies up until Howard Hughes bought out a bunch of mob hotels and saved Las Vegas, the population was approximately forty percent Mormon. Mormons founded Las Vegas and settled it. During the era when dead bodies were liberally scattered across the Las Vegas desert, the Mormons ran the city government. They commanded an impregnable voting bloc. The Clark County Sheriff was a Mormon and held that position for twenty to thirty years.

So, a bunch of mobsters ran the casino industry and stopped at nothing to protect their piece. On the other hand, you had a city full of strait-laced Mormons who consistently wanted to impose their culture and values on the town. This of course leads me into my next story.

Two big attractions led major industrial concerns to set up shop in Las Vegas. If you look on a map, Las Vegas sits between 300 to 800 miles from Denver, Boise, Laramie, Reno, Salt Lake City, Dallas, Houston, San Diego, Los Angeles, San Francisco, Portland, Seattle, and Phoenix making it a perfect distribution or shipping center in the West. This, along with its friendly tax structure, led all sorts of businesses and manufacturers to relocate to Las Vegas.

It also made sense for many upper-management types to transfer to Las Vegas to keep the business process efficient. These people jumped at the chance to come to a small city

Bruce McGimsey

with a population of 100,000. Most of these transferees had no idea of the Mormon influence or even what to expect from the Mormons. The newcomers wanted to bring in delis, all-night clubs, and cultural events, anything that gave Vegas an Eastern flair. On the flipside, the Mormons called these people outsiders. They wanted the city to be simple, conservative, strait-laced, religious, and void of outside influence. Occasionally the worlds collided.

Now here I am. I quit the casino life and moved to Utah for the sole purpose of rekindling a relationship. But I finally gave up on that idea, realizing some girls are just destined to be with losers. So I headed back to Vegas to try my luck in sales. Eventually, I strayed back into the casino business, simply because I missed the action. But first, for about three years, I completely threw myself into sales and dealing with all the newly arrived industry.

In the Las Vegas business world, a very odd phenomenon went on. Mormons, of course, ran and controlled a lot of the industry. So if you were a sales rep trying to get your foot in the door to sell your product, it behooved you to be Mormon. Or at least act like it. Mormons tended to stick together, very clannish, and only did business with each other. They used buzzwords and phrases only another Mormon understands. Of course, not every Mormon acted like this, but there were enough that it certainly hurt your bottom line if you never figured out how to crack this form of religious favoritism.

A number of businessmen and executives who were transferred to Las Vegas by their respective companies just hated it. They hated Las Vegas, they hated Mormons, and they particularly hated Mormon clannishness. The way they stuck together, imposed their religion and practices on everyone around them, and constantly worked religion into conversations gave off an aura of superiority.

At this time in Las Vegas, religion crossed over into politics, social events, sports, television, everything. To a newcomer just beginning his Las Vegas experience, this could be disconcerting to say the least. The never-ending combination of religion, purity, and goodness topped off with a thick dose of self-righteousness could drive anyone up a wall.

Especially if your normal conversations, no matter what the subject, always tilted to swearing, sex, alcohol, and violence. What I am getting to here: as a salesman, you dealt with a lot of Mormons who liked dealing only with Mormons, or you dealt with non-Mormons who refused at all costs to deal with Mormons.

So here I am, just your average salesman representing a national freight line. My job consisted of getting large companies to do their shipping through us, both inbound and outbound. Because I was trying to make a living right smack dab in the shadow of the Great White Temple, I never worried about religion. I just wanted to sell my product and bang out a living. I liked Mormons.

Time to introduce Ron, who was reputed to be one of the biggest purchasing agents in the city. All of us twenty to thirty reps vied for his business. At the time, I got a small taste from Ron but I wanted so much more. So I visited him at least half a dozen times trying to make some headway. He liked my Las Vegas stories even though he always left lots of room on my order pad after a sales call. Still, I felt a slow, gradual increase.

Ron was a small, well-built man from Philadelphia. He wanted you to believe he had been in 300 street fights growing up. "In Philly, you grow up fighting or you die." Before he moved to Las Vegas, he had no idea what a Mormon was. "Why are they so weird?" he'd ask me. "I just hate 'em."

But Ron didn't just hate them, he despised them and wanted to pick fights with them. He wanted to argue and cuss, and loved to embarrass them. So when you went to Ron's office on a sales call, his waiting area abounded with vintage Mormon no-no's, particularly ashtrays full of cigarette butts, and if he sensed a Mormon, he lit up and blew smoke in his face.

A typical Mormon's office always featured the church newspaper and possibly the National Geographic, whereas in Ron's office, you got nothing but Hustler and Playboy. Ron sent messages. He wanted to offend people, and he wanted to know it when he offended them.

So I'm waiting in Ron's office with nothing to read but Playboy Forum. Please understand I loved Playboy Forum except for the fact that the magazine conjured up the most preposterous, unbelievable stories ever written. I remember after an hour of Playboy Forum, I wondered if the same writers wrote these stories and just changed their names and addresses every month.

No matter, after an hour's wait, I got my shot at Ron. Finally, after three years of treading water in this business, I reached down and grabbed the biggest fish in the city. That day, Ron gave me more business than the rest of my customers combined—the biggest sales target in the city, and I landed him. What's more, he committed to a weekly visit. Every rep in the city wanted this customer. I had arrived!

Wow, what a great day! This, of course, called for a celebration. The problem was it was five-thirty on a Monday night in Las Vegas. At times, even I felt the frustrations that outsiders did coming here. Get off the strip, away from the tourist traps, and Vegas folded up like the Detroit Lions. Now, everyone at my office would be gone, so they couldn't share in my euphoria. I figured to be on my own to celebrate one of the best days of my young, professional career.

My office sat out by the airport in the midst of the warehouse district about a mile away from your standard conglomeration of business hotels. Even though I rarely drank, I felt this night warranted a few drinks.

About ten minutes to six, I walked through the doors of a typical business hotel lounge bar, which appeared empty. Not a single lounge chair with a body in it. Naturally, I headed for a seat at the bar when I noticed three heart stoppers turned my way staring at me with three of the biggest smiles imaginable. I literally shook my head and refocused. Are there really three beautiful women, completely turned around in their bar seats, smiling at me?

Behind them, a bartender polished glassware with a big grin on his face. I instinctively looked behind me to make sure their stare centered on me. With nobody behind me and nobody in the lounge, this called for an investigation. I reasoned if the smiles and stares faded the closer I got, I would keep walking towards the bathroom without embarrassing myself—no harm, no foul.

With the bar completely empty, the only one there to laugh

at me figured to be the bartender. Better yet, the closer I got, the better the girls looked. Even better than that, the distant glaze I'd usually get as I got closer turned into a big, "Hi, what are you doing here? When you walked through the door we thought we recognized you."

I stopped about five feet in front of them, and I'm pretty sure they didn't think of me as ugly, just as I'm absolutely positive they looked beautiful. No sooner am I searching for some kind of quality line when one of them asks me, "You are Fran Tarkington, aren't you?"

My eyes must have widened up like pancakes. I looked at the bartender for some help. He laughed and tilted his head sideways as if to say, "Go for it." The look he gave led me to think he definitely did not mistake me for Fran.

For anyone who doesn't know, Fran Tarkington played quarterback for the Minnesota Vikings during the seventies. Since his retirement, he worked as an announcer and color man on "Monday Night Football." I knew my being Fran figured to be a stretch, but I did have the same general build and his Irish chin. Plus, these girls looked so good!

So what's a salesman to do? I smiled broadly, looked around the lounge, and said, "I don't want anyone to recognize me, so don't say that too loud. I signed a business contract, and I just checked out of the Marriott across the street. At midnight I'll be catching the redeye home to Minnesota, but for now, I need to kill a little time with a few drinks." The bartender's laughter rang just short of hysterics. He put his forefinger and thumb together in a circle, giving me the okay sign, which told me this guy needed more convincing.

I never fancied myself a good-looking man. I likened myself somewhere between average and pleasant-looking. So about the best compliment I ever garnered from the opposite sex might be "He's not bad" or "He's all right." On the other hand, I knew guys who women loved. I watched the way women reacted to a good-looking man, and I knew where I stood. Still, like your stereotypical man, I wanted great-looking women with great figures, and these three filled that bill. So I decided, as farfetched and absurd as this plot seemed, I'm going for it. If I last two minutes, so be it, but if they honestly believe this

69

scenario, who knows? My first objective, get these girls away from the bartender. He seemed like the kind of guy who either had his own dreams or might even queer my action for the sheer pleasure of it.

No problem with the quality material, that seemed to work out pretty well. I relied on a few fallback lines that generally got laughs. If the girls showed personality, you hoped to take off from there, and as it turned out, these loved their fun. They liked to laugh and enjoy themselves. Some guys got it, and some guys got more of it. On this night, everything jelled. Imagine three gorgeous airline stewardesses from Minnesota on a three-day convention, bored to tears.

I talked to these three a good six or seven minutes, and everything rolled. The music from the jukebox played so loudly I felt I was screaming instead of talking. Now, picture these girls facing me with their drinks behind them on the bar. What could be better? I didn't even have to buy the first round. No sooner did I offer to buy them a drink at a corner table when "Monday Night Football" flashed on the three televisions behind the bar. The girls couldn't hear the televisions, and so long as they didn't turn around to get their drinks, they wouldn't see Fran Tarkington and Howard Cosell discussing the upcoming game.

What a problem. I'd already asked them to join me at a table, so I had to keep talking to keep them from turning around. While I'm talking, I keep looking at them, then the television, then them, then the television. The bartender smirked as my eyes bobbled up and down so much I probably reminded him of a giant yo-yo. He could hardly contain himself he laughed so hard. He unbuttoned his shirt and put his finger over his heart, flicking the material of his shirt up and down to mimic my heart beating three hundred times a minute.

I had forgotten all about "Monday Night Football" until it popped up on those TVs, but I knew that Fran and Howard always gave their pregame synopses of what each team needed to do to win. You might see Howard at halftime, reeling off his Monday night highlights of Sunday's games. You probably weren't going to see Fran again until the end of the game a good three hours later. I just needed a couple of minutes until the game started, and that would be it for his face on the monitors—stall them for two minutes tops. My gut instinct told me to run out the door and not look back. But these girls were trophies!

Finally, the telecast broke for commercial. Thank God. I knew from a hundred previous Monday night football games that when they came back from commercial, the telecast went right to kick off. With my cover still intact, I now asked the girls to grab their drinks and focused on entertaining them in the corner. The bartender wiped the imaginary sweat from his brow. It's funny now, but at the time, I didn't find him nearly as clever as he found himself.

Beautiful girls expect to be entertained, which means, keep us interested and keep us laughing. These three wanted football stories. Not about heroics, but about juicy personal stuff involving a lot of sex. They reasoned a hotshot professional quarterback must have dozens of fun, raunchy stories about what he and his teammates did on the road. One of them had read the book *Ball Four* by Jim Bouton, and I guess she thought that book pretty much summed up the way professional athletes conducted themselves. How would I know? I just knew I needed some stories.

Well, as it turned out, I had just spent an hour reading a dozen or so of Playboy Forum's most bizarre stories. I'm talking sexy, funny, and wild, but best of all, these were stories you couldn't make up, at least not right off the top of your head. Just a few creative changes to some names and NFL cities, and I turned some of the most famous Minnesota Vikings into the raunchiest sex-starved men in America. I had smut locked, loaded, and ready to fire.

Thanks to Ron, I told them story after story, and I've got to say I wowed these girls. I mean stories completely over the top, but by putting big-time superstars in them, the stories became more believable—and even better, it made them funnier. The scary thing for me, I started getting the hang of being Fran Tarkington and I liked it, especially after I offered them my elite box-seat tickets on the forty-yard line.

No matter what was going to happen, color this fun. I put all three of these girls way out of my league; nonetheless, I

Bruce McGimsey

still had a wish list. I positioned them as dream girl one, two and three, number one being my top prospect, but anyone of the three warranted consideration.

It seemed like given the chance, they might have listened to football smut for the rest of the night, but I didn't have an all-night supply. So I told them how embarrassed I'd be if these stories ever got out, and how much I'd hate having to explain myself to my teammates. I laughed at myself as I talked because I really started to believe this Fran charade. I kept wondering what actors went through when they played a role. Anyway, we agreed on one last story. Then both one and two got up and went to the ladies room, leaving me alone with number three, who sat there not engaged whatsoever. Pleasant enough, but I realized I definitely needed to cross her off the list.

A few minutes later, number two came back alone and asked if number three carried a certain brand of makeup or eyeliner. Number three popped right up and headed for the ladies room. Number two acted a lot different than number three. She slid her chair over, and within thirty seconds, we embraced in a lip lock. A confident young lady, within five or six minutes she suggested we head up to her room. Talk about a good day! As we left the lounge, the bartender gave me the thumbs up sign and off we went.

Number two's hotel room was laid out in typical standard issue. Two chairs, a table, two twin beds, Bible, television, etc. It was clean and efficient-looking, but none of that really mattered. I concerned myself with the job that lay ahead of me. After all, I had an image to live up to. I needed to represent the great Fran Tarkington. My mind's wheels turned as I set forth my plan. I will take my time, savor this night, and just possibly put in a Super Bowl performance.

A good thirty minutes later, I felt pretty good about myself. I hadn't rushed anything, and she seemed more than content. Our clothes were off, and the passion rolled, when out of the clear blue sky, in walks number one. No knock, she just walked in, headed to her bed. "Don't mind me. Sheri's only got one bed and she wanted to take a nap before we go out clubbing."

Now I'm dumbfounded! But at the same time, I'm Fran

72

Tarkington. After the load of Forum stories I'd fed these girls, a little immodesty was not supposed to shake me. No, I needed to get back in the saddle and focus.

No problems, just make a little adjustment, give things a minute or so and then bang, get back at it. No sooner did I start my groove again when I heard groaning, apparently coming from the TV. I looked back over my shoulder at the television, and slick as a whistle, number one had turned on the porn channel. When I glanced at her, she said matter-of-factly, "Well, you want me to be ready when it's my turn, don't you?" I nodded and tried to give her my wryest smile. To the beautiful woman on the next bed, who knew how that smile looked?

But it wouldn't fade, the ever-pressing thought clinging to me the rest of that night, the overpowering belief that Fran Tarkington must have the greatest life in the world. Before then, I had never really dwelled on unattainable lifestyles— what's the point? But for that night, I knew how wonderful King status felt.

Fun, nice, and these two never lost their sense of humor. Number one treated me fabulously. Adapting to this way of living could be easy. I now understood why the rich and famous always stayed in trouble.

But then the time came when I needed to get dressed, go home, and try and recreate every detail in my mind. I wanted to re-enact this day and store it in my memory bank forever. That way I'd be able to recall this night over and over and over. So as I'm getting dressed and trying to stay in character, I thought I detected a little note of sarcasm from the girls. I'm feeling so good about this day, do I really want to press this? If my cover's blown, I'm going to want to skedaddle as fast as I can. But curiosity got the best of me, and I ended up asking them what's up.

Now, understand that I thought I had turned in a Pro Bowl winning performance tonight. Not just yeoman's work, but a job that would have every one of my Viking teammates exchanging high fives with me. In fact, I was so proud of my sexual prowess that I thought I might even finally hear those words that every man covets at least once in his lifetime. Any second I figured one of these two cuties to proclaim, "Wow, Fran. That was wonderful. I think I saw God tonight."

I honestly felt I had broken these two off a piece of celestial bliss, that I had given them a preview of heaven. Instead, I got sarcasm. Color me confused. Instinctively, I almost took back the box seats I offered them for the next game, but I liked to put Fran Tarkington above that sort of pettiness. If I blew my cover, so be it.

Number one looked at me with her ever-engaging smile. "Come on. We know you're not Fran Tarkington."

"What are you talking about?"

"We were bored stiff. So we started playing this game we always play. When someone walks by we guess what celebrity they look like."

Now, number two chimes in. "Sometimes it's close, sometimes we're not even in the ballpark. Before you walked in, we'd already seen Johnny Carson, Barbra Streisand, and Walter Cronkite."

"You knew all along?"

"Exactly, quick-draw, why do you think we were laughing so hard when you walked in? Even that smartass bartender thought it was funny."

"Oh yeah, you didn't like him either."

"Hell no, that guy was a jerk."

"You saved us, that alone scored you big points. But we never dreamt you were going to play along."

"Then we kept egging you on," number one says, "just to see how far you'd go, and when Fran showed up on TV, you didn't even bat an eye. I don't know if I've ever met anyone that quick-witted before."

"You knew Fran Tarkington was on TV and didn't you say anything?"

"We were having fun, you idiot."

Number one then asks, "How did you come up with those stories?"

"I figured I had a shot if I kept talking."

"But you never wavered, one story after another, just like it happened yesterday. Did that come right off the top of your head?"

"I was thinking, no stories, game over."

"Those stories were unbelievable."

Number two then asks, "Did any of that stuff happen, or did you make it all up?"

"You think any of that could really happen to anyone?"

Number one, "Well, it was so spontaneous, we were impressed. We wanted to ask you to go to a nightclub with us, but Terri and I knew we would end up fighting over you. So we devised this little plan in the ladies room. We figured we'd both have you. I hope you're not embarrassed. We didn't know if it would be better to tell you or let you believe you fooled us."

I was dying to ask them a few questions about my self-perceived sexual prowess, but what if I didn't like the answers? Nope, for a few hours, I really was Fran Tarkington, and the smartest thing I could do now was bid them farewell and try and rethink everything that happened on this day so I could replay it my mind anytime I wanted too.

Oh yeah, life was sweet after all.

She Loves Me,
She Loves Me Not

Okay, I'm thirty-two years old and beginning to see my marriage prospects grow dimmer and dimmer. I have to admit that the idea of living out the rest of my life alone bothered me, a lot. Nevertheless, so far I'd never found anyone who loved me. In fact, I'd never even heard the words, "Bruce, I love you."

I worked as a food and beverage troubleshooter for a Las Vegas corporation that owned a string of hotels, and had been out of dealing for three or four years. I flew all over the country staying in various suspect hotels trying to resolve their food and/or beverage problems. It was a good job and I probably had a future with this corporation. Then my old sidekick, Big Dave, gave me a call.

Understand, Dave and I had already collaborated in a restaurant five years earlier, a total disaster that folded in six months.

Anyway, Dave wanted me to partner up again with him in a club in Ogden, Utah. He had his eye on a restaurant and lounge with a separate liquor license. Getting this going in Ogden, Utah, was no small feat, but he had it figured pretty well. The place stood in an old historic part of town, and the city offered us a loan at half a percent interest if we used their design in remodeling. What a deal!

For me, the ever-pressing desire to be a big shot consumed me, and this was a great opportunity. I quit my job, and six months later, we opened up our private club in Utah.

Praise to the business Gods, this place jumped. From

Bruce McGimsey

day one, we rocked, and I'm not sure why, but who cares? Success! Besides success, we loved the fun. Even on my days off, I ended up back at our joint because the trendy people gathered there first.

Instead of your standard ladies' night special, we had sluts' night. All sluts drank free with one small caveat. To get free drinks, first you stepped up to the microphone and introduced yourself. "Hello, my name is so-and-so!" Then, à la Alcoholics Anonymous, the crowd would chant, "Hello, so-and-so." Then, of course, to the crowd's glee, so-and-so also had to say, "And I'm a slut." For the college kids, this went over like whiskey at an Irish wake.

Now, my number-one purpose in life was to be rich, and if it took hard work to attain that goal, so be it. That meant I tried a little bit of everything: bartending, cooking, waiting tables, whatever it took to make the place tick. Seventy-five percent of our business was under thirty years old, and at that time I'm kicking thirty-three right in the ass. Consequently, I never looked at our female customers as potential love interests simply because too many young stallions galloped and strutted around the place. To me, if we attracted and then held the girls who walked in the door, we'd get that many more guys coming in and spending their money. So, everybody knew the rule. Offend the ladies by hitting on them, and you risked chasing them away. Chase the girls away and we all lose.

Lorie walked in the first night, but because of the rule, I never paid much attention. She rated as an arm piece and maybe a heart stopper. But for me, she looked like a dollar sign so long as we treated her right. It never struck me as odd that every time I walked by her, she smiled and interrupted the Adonis hovering around her to talk to me. Ah, a friendly girl! That's got to be good for business.

What did strike me as odd was that this went on for eight or nine days straight. Finally, my partner and some of the waitresses urged me to give her a shot, she's interested. My first response—why? How could she possibly be interested in me? She's probably ten years younger, great-looking, and every guy in the place pursued her. Then again, nothing

78

ventured, nothing gained—and nothing to lose, except of course a little pride and maybe a lot of money.

Finally, at the end of the night, I approached her. I sat down, introduced myself, and within ten minutes, she got me feeling as if I was in a league of my own. She offered better lines than the standard, "You look better than all these young guys here." She led me to believe that my combination of class and character rendered all those other guys helpless.

But do I buy it? Of course I do! No red flags were raised, no self-doubt, no wondering how she surmised all this in a week's worth of watching me and ten minutes of conversation. Nope, if you're pretty, ten minutes of stroking my ego and you own me.

Within a couple of weeks, we were an item. Within a couple of months, we might as well have been married, we were together so much. Overall, I liked it. We got along great. She treated me like a prince, and I rarely got jealous of her because she never put me in that position. Nonetheless, we lived apart and I never gave her a key to my apartment. I lacked that feeling of burning love, and I'm really not sure why.

Anyway, one day four or five months up the road, I came home to my apartment looking for some paperwork. I searched for it in an obscure place in the bottom drawer of a desk that I used for such paperwork. Lo and behold, I ran into this zippered notebook that I'd never seen before. Odd, what's this doing here? Of course I investigated, and to my amazement, it turned into a succession of paperwork with a blank check of mine and a blank check of Lorie's. Lorie had cut up my check and her check, then pasted them together, copied them, and repeated the process, again repeated the process, until finally there was one perfect looking check. The end result reading, Bruce and Lorie McGimsey, with my address, my phone number and my account number.

A head scratcher to say the least. What mischievous deed had she conjured up with this check? What could she do? How did she get into my place? Where did she learn how to do this and do it so well? They seemed like relevant questions to me. They also seemed like questions that needed answers, now!

Bruce McGimsey

After I called the bank to make sure I still had money in my account, I decided to play the diligent boyfriend. So I called Lorie and asked her to come see me, posthaste. What line of questioning should I pursue? Maybe show her the evidence and ask her to confess? Alternatively, maybe show her nothing and try to trick her? The lingering problem with that play, she might be smarter than me.

She finally got to my place and my anger got the better of me. I immediately showed her everything and asked her for answers. Her first response was to ask me what was I doing nosing around in her paperwork?

"Nice try, Lorie, but half of it is my paperwork. This is a deal breaker, and I need to know what it's all about."

She thought for a while, obviously flustered, then began to cry. She mustered up this gem, and I quote: "Okay, Bruce, you've got me. I love you and loved you since the first day I met you. It doesn't seem like you'll ever ask me to marry you. So I just started dreaming about what my name would look like as Lorie McGimsey. All women do this when they find the one. I'm sorry!"

All these years later, that little act sounded pretty weak. But there's something you need to understand here. Nobody, and I mean not a single girlfriend, date, friend, or acquaintance, had ever told me they loved me. So, sure enough, right on the spot, I asked her to marry me. I refrained from asking her any more tough questions. So, did I just step into a wonderful lifetime partnership or a lifetime nightmare?

I figured out much too late that this check enabled her to go to my bank, act like she was going to write a check at the teller's window, then proclaim she wasn't sure if the money in the account covered the check. Now she could conveniently ask the teller, "Will you check? Oh, and by the way, how much do I have in savings?"

I thought we probably needed a couple of months before we hitched up. Hardly. She wanted us married without any ceremony and figured to get this wedding thing done in about four days. To my surprise, she told me not to worry about a ring. Now, with no financial worries, somehow I felt less committed. Obviously, she read me like a second-grade primer, but at the time, it seemed like such a deal. So I wimped out and married her four days later. Did I really love her? That's another question.

For the next three or four months, things went great. We got along and everything sailed nicely. My pessimism and doubt slowly evaporated, which left only one problem, my business partner's attitude. The club thrived, but he just didn't think the money stretched out enough for both of us to get fat. Consequently, we agreed one of us needed to go. So we decided on a fair price, flipped a coin, and the winner bought out the loser.

Surprise, surprise, I lost. We had negotiated a fair price, and I stood to make a nice profit after only a year's time. It took me about a week to find a job as a casino food and beverage manager in a small northern Nevada town. So off we went—me, Lorie, and our dog, Rodog.

After about four months counting cattle trucks roaring past us on the highway, this little town made us both stir crazy. So I found a job in Sacramento with a hotel chain, doing food and beverage, and we hit the road again.

It was then I received the biggest clue yet that Lorie thought outside the box. All packed up, ready for our trip, Lorie tossed me the keys to her new 280ZX. She wanted me to take her car while she drove my little fifteen-year-old piece of junk. Lorie never let anyone drive her car. She even took Rodog with her. Perplexed, I accepted her gracious offer.

As it turned out, the trip went smoothly. We checked in at my future employer's hotel, ready to work. The next morning while my boss ironed out my schedule, Lorie went to the bank to open up our new checking account.

Then things got sticky. While in my boss's office, Lorie called me in tears. She told me her 280ZX had just been stolen but she couldn't call the cops. "Of course you can call the cops, and if you don't, I will." My boss leaned in so as not to miss a word, so I told him that somebody had just stolen my wife's car. Lorie overheard me tell the boss and proceeded to give me a tongue-lashing for telling him. This in turn made me mad. I told her I'd meet her at the bank in five minutes.

At the bank, Lorie tells me she couldn't call the cops

Bruce McGimsey

because her car was already stolen. She bought the car hot and had the two most convenient serial numbers changed. Now I understood why she so graciously allowed me to drive her car on our trip. If by chance I got stopped, driving a stolen car across state lines became a federal beef, which made the charges more serious. So if the police did pull me over, she and Rodog would wave as they passed me by, never to be seen again.

It bothered me that she drove a stolen car but worse yet, she knew people who dealt in stolen cars. Plus she knew people who changed serial numbers and apparently knew how to make a hot car appear legal.

What to do? Probably get the hell out of this marriage. There were certainly enough clues that spelled slick. I never wanted slick when looking for a wife. We lived on my money exclusively ever since we'd wed. She never contributed a dime, her excuse being that since I never bought her a ring, that equaled money saved.

I ended up quitting the job in Sacramento and we headed for Vegas. Since I grew up in Las Vegas, I planned to start anew, get a job in one of the casinos, and get my young, good-looking wife into serving cocktails or maybe working as a camera girl.

It took about a week for the plan to come together. I got a job in food and beverage in one of the casinos. Instead of serving cocktails, Lorie got a job as a junior executive accountant for a highfaluting accounting firm. I never even knew she'd gone to college.

She then offered to open up a checking account and put five thousand dollars in it. "Listen," she said, "I understood that you've paid the freight since we met, and it's only fair for me to start pulling my own weight."

I signed a few papers for our joint account and she made good on the money. She went down to the bank and opened up a joint checking account the next day. She even kept the account at five thousand over the next few months. Okay, credit given, but where did she get five grand?

Things were good with the exception of one telltale sign. My father despised her, which gave Lorie the kiss of death.

82

My father always delivered good, sound advice. If I did not heed his advice, I never heard "I told you so." He never gloated. It just seemed like he never, ever steered me wrong. If I followed another direction, it didn't always mean things went sour. It just meant I could be in for trouble.

Lorie and I went fine for about three or four months. I worked nights and got off at one in the morning. She worked strictly eight to five. One morning, I got a call from my credit card company from a lady asking for Lorie. When I said she wasn't here, the lady remarked how odd that was, because she had just talked to Lorie and she gave this as her callback number. I asked the lady for an explanation. She asked if I knew Lorie had maxed out my credit card for $10,000. What's more, she received cash at a casino, so they charged me ten percent—so much for my $11,000 credit limit.

Ouch! I hung up and called my other two credit card companies. Sure enough, she maxed those out too, all in the same night. She obviously eased the cards out of my wallet while I slept, collected the money at the casinos, and who knew what else?

Ironically, I never used credit cards. I carried them at my father's suggestion, trying to build my credit rating. Whenever I bought something with them, I always paid off the balance each month, which explained my high limits. What I didn't understand was why Lorie told the credit card lady to call her back at home, as if she wanted me to find out.

So, I went off to work that day and made arrangements to come home and discuss things with my ever-loving wife. I confronted her early that evening. She apologized and admitted she had a gambling problem. Once she got down so far, she started doubling down her bets, trying to win it back. She never revealed any logical answer as to why she needed all three credit cards.

No matter. I told her I needed to end it and would get the divorce going with a lawyer brother of mine. Of course, she swore to pay back every penny.

I agonized all that night at work, and when I finally got home, I agonized in bed all night trying to sleep. It seemed like no sooner had I fallen asleep when a process server with

Bruce McGimsey

divorce papers knocked on my door. Lorie had started the ball rolling a week earlier with her own lawyer. She wanted me to find out about the credit cards so I'd ask her for a divorce. What a piece of work! I signed the paperwork in a completely confused state.

I tried to get back to sleep, but after two hours, one little detail haunted me. So I jumped up and called my bank requesting savings account information. I knew she'd empty the checking account, but the savings account was in my name only, or so I thought. It turned out, the reason she volunteered to open up a checking account using her money was to get me to sign paperwork. She snuck my savings account into the transaction and the banking lady thought nothing of it. After all, we were married.

All told, she got me for my life savings—all the money I made from selling my half of the club, and credit card debt ringing up at thirty-three grand. Approximately one hundred thousand dollars lost. Talk about bad karma. But the truth was that Lorie had sent up enough red flags to agitate every bull in Spain.

Karma Owes Me

Does everyone play hold 'em these days? Okay, after my ex-wife had beaten me out of my nest egg, I constantly looked for a way to get it back. Who wouldn't? The only problem, I had no get-rich-quick schemes. For sure I didn't have the brain or the heart to rob a bank. I was never going to pull off some major score illegally.

Out of nowhere, enters Tam, a big-mouthed obnoxious Italian from New York—you know, "from the neighborhood," your stereotypical New York Italian mafia wannabe, a guy who had a friend who had a friend who was connected. This guy wore shoes that always matched the color of his suits (green suit, green shoes, grey suit, grey shoes, etc.). Before Tam, I never knew anyone who owned a pair of green shoes. How in the hell would you even know where to buy a pair of green shoes? Plus, these New Yorkers seemed to have a very bigoted mindset. They would refer to the PR or Puerto Rican problem in New York, or maybe the Mick or Irish problem. Well, in Las Vegas, we always referred to New Yorkers as the New York problem, people who thought they were special or with it simply because they were from New York. If you weren't one of them, you were a potential sucker.

Anyway, one weekend, while visiting my old pool-hustling buddies in Salt Lake City, I found out a group of Las Vegans had made a special trip to match up with my pool-playing friends. This party might happen twice a year, in either Salt Lake City or Las Vegas. The sets of guys squared off and played for hours, generally consuming a whole weekend. By the end of the day, no hard feelings, just if you lost, next time

85

Bruce McGimsey

get yourself a better bet.

I hung out at the local players bar, making a few side bets. Everything's cool, the Vegas guys loved to gamble, and I enjoyed getting to know these guys, when out of the clear blue, Tam, the pain-in-the-ass New Yorker, completely went off on one of my friends, accusing him of cheating in their nine-ball game. On top of that, he started calling my buddy a sleazy Mexican and talking about the "Mexican problem" that permeated Las Vegas. Needless to say, fisticuffs loomed.

Tam was way overmatched and didn't know it. I interceded and finally got cooler heads to prevail. But my first introduction to Tam left me extremely unimpressed, to say the least. For me and all my misgivings about New York Italians, the only thing off-key was Tam's name. He should have been Vinnie or Rocco. Anyway, we ended up agreeing that no money would change hands. The real story here, I didn't much care for Tam. He refused to apologize. Like a little baby, he also refused to play anymore. I got the feeling that Tam never apologized to anyone.

Later on that night, I had another exchange with Tam. The barmaid, Wendy, showed up at our table to offer last call for drinks. There had to be ten of us sitting around this table when Wendy asked her standard rhetorical question. "Last call, how's everybody doing?"

Without hesitation, Tam said, "Funny you should ask. I got a heartbreaking story to tell you. You got a few minutes after work for me?"

Amazingly, Wendy answered, "Sure, I do."

Now Wendy was an absolute cutie. It astounded me that Tam took his shot with her in front of nine witnesses. I turned to Tam. "Does that weak line always work?"

"Hey, I'm a great looking guy, looks and audacity are a major part of my game. When you look this good, you don't have to be witty, just don't be obnoxious." I'd never forget that statement.

Six or seven months later, a different friend, but one of the guys who had witnessed Tam's explosion on my buddy, came down from Salt Lake to visit me in Las Vegas. We were hanging around in one of the casinos when we ran into Tam.

86

Since I didn't care for him, I said hello, shook his hand, and made up some excuse to leave. As it turned out, Tam was a poker dealer just waiting to start his shift. A few minutes later, I hooked back up with my friend. He told me Tam had made him a great offer.

It seemed he had this grandiose scheme of cheating a poker table out of big money. The plan focused not on cheating the casino but on cheating the other players at the table. My friend asked me if this guy could really pull it off. Are there card mechanics so good that nobody can spot them? Apparently. Tam bragged about his skills, so I told my friend a story about the old twenty-one dealer who showed up out of nowhere and beat a player out of two hundred grand, only to disappear and never be seen again. This interested my friend, but he really didn't have the fiber for this kind of intrigue. Besides, he lived in Utah.

I kicked this around in my head for a few days and finally decided that karma owed me. So a few nights later, I headed out to the same casino and conveniently ran into Tam. We talked awhile and sure enough, Tam ended up making me the same offer to be part of his poker table cheating scam.

Tam would deal a hold 'em game that had either a twenty or a forty-dollar limit, and sometimes dealt a no-limit game. Both games could get real expensive in a hurry. His plan was that every time I mucked my two hole cards, those same two cards would be the first two cards flopped on the very next hand.

Now in hold 'em, all players keep two hole cards face down. You then passed, bet, or folded. Next, the dealer deals three cards up in the middle of the table, known as the "flop." They are community cards that everyone can and must use. So if your hole cards are a pair of tens, and the dealer flops an ace, jack, and eight of spades, you've got an ace, jack, eight, and pair of tens. After the flop, you bet, pass or fold once again, and then a fourth community card, called the "river," gets dealt face up. Another round of betting happens, and a fifth and final card is dealt face up. Each player is then obligated to use his two hole cards along with three of the five community cards. You now make final bets and a winner gets determined.

Bruce McGimsey

So if you happen to know what those first two community cards are going to be without having to pay for them, you have a huge betting edge on the other players. Even an amateur should win. But on top of this, I had a dealer who could underhandedly deal any card he wanted on the last turn, just in case other players in the game appeared to have me beat.

Tam loved this scenario because he thought nobody would suspect that a hip guy like him and a square like me would hook up to rip off a game. Talk about New York obnoxious, Tam had insulted me and asked me to partner up all in the same sentence.

The first night we discussed his plan, he put on an amazing display of card-dealing magic. But even with his skills, he had one main concern, the eye in the sky, aka casino surveillance. I knew that the eye in the sky never paid attention to poker rooms simply because they never made casinos enough money. Their worries centered on the table games and slot machines. What did they care about lowlife poker players cheating each other? The casino I worked at would not even watch a bartender I suspected of stealing. The most I got from our eye in the sky people, maybe they would set a camera on him and make a tape of his shift. I would then have to wade through hours of tape and try to catch the bartender's moves on my own.

But what really sold Tam on this idea was the fact that another poker dealer in his room stole and got away with it. He dealt a 3-6 hold 'em game, and every time he pushed a pot to a winner, he would cuff a chip between his thumb and the palm of his hand. Then he waited until the winner tipped him a chip or two, a customary move on the poker scene, scooped up his tip along with his ill-gotten cuffed chip, and dropped them both into his left shirt pocket, standard procedure for a poker dealer receiving a tip. He made this move on every pot over $15, all night long.

When I pointed this out to Tam, he could not believe it until he saw it with his own eyes. So first chance he got, he watched the guy do it over and over again. It impressed Tam that a square like me spotted this move when he hadn't after working with the guy for months. The next morning, we ate breakfast and set forth the plan.

Playing hold 'em with players a lot better than me could certainly be intimidating. But I have to admit, as nerve wracking as it was cheating in a Las Vegas casino, it also became intoxicating. These guys got so mad when you beat them. They would slam their cards down and ask me how I ever played those rags in the first place. Then they would tell me just to keep it up and they would bust me. Hold 'em players can be both smug and obnoxious. Just watch them on television for half an hour. At least half the players I played fancied themselves professionals. On any given night, everybody in the game knew they played better than me. So when they explained to me how much I needed to learn, I simply agreed with them and explained how lucky they were to have a sucker like me willing to donate to them. I did need to win once in a while or I wouldn't want to come back.

The funniest thing about this arrangement, besides the money, was that my opponents thought I was an idiot. One night, while knee-deep in a no-limit game, Tam interrupted two players discussing the last hand. He said to the one player, "Sharkey, if you believe he had trip Kings, I will sell you the Brooklyn Bridge."

So, with the straightest face I could muster, I said loud enough for the whole table to hear, "What are you talking about? I already own the Brooklyn Bridge." I was only kidding, but there seemed to be such a lack of respect for me that this guy and the other self-proclaimed big shots believed me. I added, "I didn't buy it alone. We're a conglomeration, and I've got a receipt from the state to prove it."

Sharkey said, "I'd like to see that receipt. Does it have an official New York seal?"

"Of course I got the State seal, and the State Treasurer's signature. What do you think, I'm an idiot?" Laughter erupted from the table.

Tam and I actually became good friends, which of course gave me pause about my theory of the New York problem. Our only disagreement stemmed from how long we should go on doing this. I wanted out, and Tam wanted to continue indefinitely. As much as I loved beating these conceited, self-indulgent hold 'em players, I was cheating. In a fair game, my limit might be two hours with these guys before they busted me. Plus, if we ever did get caught, we'd never work in a casino again. So, we compromised and settled on one more month. At first, I played once a week then made it twice a week.

I always met Tam the next day to cut up the loot. On occasion, he gave me a tip that I had a "tell", which meant that the other players could read me when I had a good hand. Or he might brief me as to how I should have played a hand to win more money. Since Tam always knew my hand, and because of the first two cards flopped, he occasionally gave me a river card to win a big hand. I also made a point to be cheap when I tipped him during the course of the night so that when I left the table on bathroom breaks, he could badmouth me to the other players. That way, he got inside information on what they thought.

Everything seemed to be going great. We had to force ourselves not to get too greedy and play too often. On occasion, I might even skip playing for a couple of weeks just to stay away from patterns. Finally, one night right when Tam was waiting for the break dealer to finish dealing his last hand, a phalanx of FBI agents and state gaming control agents surrounded us, barking out commands.

"Men, everyone keep your hands on the table where we can keep track of them."

"Why, what did we do?"

"We'll get to that later. For now, we're confiscating all the chips at this table."

"You can't do that!"

"Oh yeah? Watch us. We'll be investigating some alleged improprieties going on at this table. Once we sort this out, anyone not involved will get his money back." I looked at Tam and wondered if I looked as scared as he did. That aura of confidence he constantly maintained had vanished. He looked at me as if he were trying to send me messages through our shared extrasensory perception. We figured we knew what this was all about. What happened next perplexed us.

"Stand up," the agent said to the break dealer, "put your hands behind your back, we're arresting you. These are your rights." He then emptied the dealer's shirt pocket onto the table. "Do you think this is a lot of money in tips? Do any of you remember tipping any twenty-five dollar chips? I didn't think so."

A different agent told us, "We're going to take you upstairs and interview you one at a time. Once you're all cleared, you'll be welcome to come back and continue your poker game."

As it turned out, this was the dealer I'd spotted a year ago cuffing chips from the pots he pushed to winning players. We knew he never stopped that sleazy chip move, but we couldn't do anything about it. If we complained, it would have brought down undue heat on us. Apparently, someone else complained, and they'd been watching this guy for weeks. Fortunately for us, he rarely broke the high-stakes poker games, or the investigation would have undoubtedly stumbled into our little scam.

So we spent half the night anguishing over our plight, thinking that the display of high-powered agents couldn't just be about one dealer cuffing chips. But as far as we knew, that was it exactly. Some of the agent's statements and then later on some things the poker bosses said to Tam made us suspicious. Were they onto us? Or maybe we were just paranoid. One way or another, I couldn't handle the anxiety.

Finally, between the risks we took and not being able to rationalize doing this anymore, I quit cold turkey. I just couldn't justify it any longer. This certainly was not a proud time in my life, but it happened. I never saw Tam again. Nor did I ever hear of him. I just hope his bones are not bleached out in the desert somewhere. I surely wish him well and I no longer believed that Karma owed me.

Bruce McGimsey

Can Anyone
Get This Lucky?

Somewhere between my thirtieth and thirty-fifth birthday, I peaked in the looks department, certainly not handsome but possibly above average. Anyway, I knew my looks were headed downhill, and after my marriage fiasco, I figured maybe I needed to broaden my standards.

One day, a police friend called me with a dilemma. "Bruce, my partner's sister just moved to town, and he needs to find her a nice guy. Since you're the only nice guy I know, and my partner is driving me crazy, I need your help on this one." I recommended another cop, but my friend said absolutely not. "Cops are not nice guys."

Like most men, I hated blind dates. I never had any luck with this sort of thing, and I really didn't want to do it. But my friend begged me, and after all, he was a cop. For a guy like me, an appreciative cop might come in handy someday. So I told him to give me the sister's number, and I'd call her that night, regardless of the bad feeling lingering in my stomach.

That night, Lindsay expected my call, so the conversation flowed well enough. We didn't get into global politics or the state of our economy, and everything stayed on a simple level. She had moved here with her best friend and roommate, Suzie Beau. They were both eighth-grade teachers from Kansas. They had bought new cars the same day at the same place. Their dog's name was Spiker. She hated Chinese food.

This went on for an hour. I learned all sorts of trivial details about her life and her roommate's life because that's the way a conversation like this goes. Finally, she told me her whole

92

name, Lindsay Snow. The two of them together were Lindsay Snow and Suzie Beau. She told me they got tired of the stupid comments people made about their rhyming names. I assured her I was above that kind of adolescent humor (as I chuckled to myself).

We decided to meet. She would bring her roommate, Suzie, and I would bring my friend Larry. We planned a rendezvous on Friday night at a seafood buffet in a casino. She wanted me to wear a bright red sweater so she wouldn't have to walk around looking for me. Does this seem like a strange request? At the time, I thought not, but the next day, Larry warned me that the red sweater spelled trouble.

Larry, a lifelong friend, reasoned that a good laugh took precedence over everything else, no matter what the expense or the consequences. If feelings got hurt or the intended laugh never materialized, you just moved on. So when Larry cautioned me about wearing the red sweater, I figured Larry for a few laughs at my expense. His theory was that red sweaters stick out like honest lawyers at a car sales convention. As scary as I looked, once the girls focused on me, they'd scatter. He honed in on the idea of him wearing the red sweater, insisting that his looks wouldn't scare the girls away, whereas one glimpse of me from afar and goodbye, ladies. In my opinion, I felt my looks outclassed Larry's, and this just gave him a chance to rough me up in a department in which he could not compete.

Friday night rolled up, and like an idiot, I'm in my bright red sweater. Buffets are generally cheap in Las Vegas, but a Friday-night seafood buffet rang up at $25 apiece. "Bruce," Larry theorized, "your party, your money, and if that's a problem, I'll leave." Thus, I coughed up a $100 bill. At buffets, you pay up front, so we sat down and anxiously readied ourselves for Lindsay Snow and Suzie Beau. Larry loved the thought of goofing on these two.

We waited and waited while Larry ate and ate, until about half an hour later, when I heard my name paged over the hotel intercom system. Between bites, Larry wisecracked, "I knew it. I told you not to wear the sweater. She got one look at you and left." As I headed out of the buffet toward a house phone, I heard "Bad Moon Rising" blaring from the lounge

Bruce McGimsey

act performing on the other side of the casino. When I picked up the house phone, I still heard "Bad Moon Rising" over the phone, meaning this call came from inside the hotel.

"Bruce, this is Lindsay. I can't make it tonight. I'm so sick I can't even get out of bed. How about I give you a call next week?"

"Yeah, sure," I said and hung up. Was I disgusted. She'd arrived, scoped me out from a distance, and decided Bruce was too ugly to share a free seafood buffet. Old hideous-looking Bruce couldn't be confronted face to face. The two women must have spotted a repulsive looking guy like me from twenty yards away. After all, we'd been searching for two women in their late twenties and saw no one even close. So either they brought binoculars or detected my gruesome looks from way back. I wager that if she saw me again, she wouldn't recognize me. How could she? She never got close enough.

I was steaming. I went back to the table as Larry was about to start his third trip to the buffet. "Apparently, I'm too repugnant to be seen with."

"I could have told you that before you blew a hundred bucks. Hey, forget about it, the food's great."

I couldn't forget about it, but what could I do? Her brother's a cop. I couldn't call her back for fear of retribution. Was I mad? Do fat dogs fart? Nonetheless, calling my police friend back to ream him out would only make me sound petty. I had no out. Nope, I needed to eat this, so that's exactly what I did.

A year passed, and Larry and I were at T.G.I. Friday's for dinner before a movie. T.G.I. Friday's sat on levels, so you really felt like you were on top of one another. We heard six conversations going on around us at a time. With the place packed, the manager came up to us and said, "The only two empty seats in the house are at your table, would you mind if I sat two young ladies with you?"

We were in a good mood, having a great time talking to the four ladies seated next to us, and said, "Why not? Bring 'em."

The four girls next to us were heart-stoppers; not only were they out of our league, but normally we'd never even find the ball field they played on. But you get up to bat, swing for the

94

fences, and every once in a while you make contact. Ever hear the saying, "Some guys got it and some guys got more of it?" Well, on this particular night, I owned it, I was in the zone. Everything I said lay out like silk. Not only did I have these girls in phone number mode, but all the tables around us had zeroed in on my two-step. Larry sensed good things in the works. Two more ladies in the mix could only bring a bigger audience to showcase my batting skills.

The manager brought the pair to our table. They sat down, and within thirty seconds, they closed their menus. One of them thanked me for allowing them to share our table then introduced herself as Lindsay and her friend as Suzie.

Wow! I had to take a shot here. I put one hand on my forehead as if in deep concentration and closed my eyes. "Don't tell me. I've got you read." I gave it about five seconds. "Let me guess...school teachers from Kansas?"

They gasped, smiled simultaneously, and asked in stereo, "How did you know that?"

Holy hell, could anyone get this lucky? Thank you, Jesus!

"Ladies, I'm a mind reader. I work at the Follies, a review for one of the Strip hotels."

Suzie said, "I don't believe you. That stuff's all fake."

"Fake? We'll see." I introduced myself as Allen, my middle name, then introduced Larry. I told them my stage name was The Great Zambucu, which not only made them laugh, but also made the four ladies we were previously talking to laugh. Plus the seven tables eavesdropping also enjoyed a chuckle. Even my friend Larry giggled.

"I'll ask you questions," I said, "that subconsciously make you think of the answers. That way, even if you try to think of wrong answers, your subconscious will think correctly and I'm good enough to detect it." Having previously spent an hour on the phone finding out trivial details about these two, I felt pretty confident. I never forgot those details, just as I never forgot how these two stood us up on that blind date.

Larry appeared clueless. He looked at me in sheer disbelief but did have a wry smile on his face as if to say, "I can't wait to see where you take this." Right then, my mind clicked so fast I was afraid my ears were smoking.

Bruce McGimsey

I started out asking them, then telling them, the colors of their cars, their dog's name, what grade they taught, and finally, their last names. With this, Larry caught on and couldn't contain himself. He leaned over to them and said, "Let me get this straight. You're Lindsay Snow and Suzie Beau?"

Lindsay half-heartedly snarled back, "Yeah, yeah, so what?"

Larry just laughed and at the same time shook his head. Can anyone get this lucky?

Of the two girls, Suzie seemed the less personable, so I most enjoyed sticking the needle to her. "Sometimes you're hard to read because your mind can be a complete fog. Do your students ever pick up on that?"

"Oh yeah," she said, "they think I'm downright stupid."

All the tables around me were in awe. Nobody laughed at The Great Zambucu now. From a table two rows above me some guy yelled out, "Guess what my name is."

I smiled. "Look, folks, I've got two beautiful women here at my table, and I've got their wholehearted attention. Please, let me focus." Of course what I really thought was, who are these two gals kidding, at best they rated a notch above average. The chutzpah!

One of the tables on the opposite side yelled out, "Do you ever work with the police?"

Lindsay chimed in, "Yeah, my brother's a cop."

I turned to her and wiped off the faint grin I wore since starting my act. With the most serious face I had, I said, "I used to work with them, but one detective berated me and called me the Voodoo King. Until he starts appreciating this gift I've been blessed with, I won't help them anymore. They can use their lie detectors to see if their suspects are lying."

This turned out to be Larry's favorite line of the night. He about busted a gut. He leaned over and pretended to tie his shoe, trying to hide his laughter. Still, as much fun as this was, our movie start time approached. So, the question was, am I through with these two? How cruel am I capable of being? When does a fun little payback become vicious and petty?

For me, apparently never. I thought about the $100 buffet, how I was too ugly to be seen with, how I'd worn that stupid bright red sweater, and to add insult to insult, I'd listened to Larry's cracks the rest of that night. Was I done with these two? Hardly! A year earlier Lindsey had taken the steam right out of my fastball. Vengeance shall be mine, sayeth the Lor—excuse me, sayeth The Great Zambucu.

Right before we left the table, I told them what good sports they were. "Most girls would be intimidated if a guy had read them like a third-grade storybook. But since you two have been so pleasant about this, why don't you be my guests at the show tomorrow night? The show, food, beverages, and even the tips will go on my comp. I haven't used my comp privileges in months, so don't worry about cost. You won't be taking advantage. Just have anything on the menu, and don't bother waiting in line. The maître d' will be expecting you."

These two loved it. "What time?" they asked. "Can we really order anything we want?" And the topper, "Are you going to put us in the act?"

I assured them the sky was the limit and that they wouldn't be taking advantage. But I'd never use them in my act because that was cheating, and I never cheat.

Our heart-stoppers, the four Rockettes who'd listened to me for the last hour, were also asking for a freebie. Larry, now in complete giggle mode, urged me to invite them to the show too. He got so caught up in this charade he couldn't wait to hear what I might say next.

I explained to the four women that management frowned on too many comps in one night, but I'd be glad to do it if they'd call me any day the following week. I gave them my phone number and my middle name. They seemed to buy it, but I shot a stern look at Larry, which of course just made him giggle more.

It just so happened that at the hotel where The Follies played, I knew a friend in a position to help me. Gary, who used to be my boss, now managed the food and beverage department at that hotel, and I had taken his old job as the food and beverage director at my establishment. Favors like comps were easy and exactly the way Vegas worked.

Bruce McGimsey

I gave Gary a call the next day and told him I needed two passes to get into the show. I wouldn't need food and beverage comped, just the passes. I'd be around earlier that evening with $20 for the maître d' and $20 for the waiter. I wanted the two ladies to sit stage side but the maître d' was not to accept a gratuity from them. Gary asked, "What's up?" and I explained my plan. He laughed. "You know, this is vintage Bruce!"

The next night went down like a six-inch putt. The girls cut right through the line straight to the podium. The maître d' seated them stage side and didn't accept their tip. Sure enough, just like I hoped, the girls never bothered to check with their waiter about a comp. Waiters never question orders. The bigger the order, the bigger the tip.

These two ordered the most expensive champagne on the menu and rang up the bill to more than five hundred dollars. They apparently didn't panic, even when "The Great Zambucu" never materialized. They asked the waiter about Zambucu during the floorshow, but he just gave them an odd look.

At the end of the show, the waiter brought them their bill. First, they wanted to know where to sign. The waiter told them that in order to sign, they needed a credit card, otherwise they would have to pay cash. Now panic set in, and when they explained that "The Great Zambucu" comped them, the waiter laughed hysterically until it occurred to him that these two women were serious.

The girls never even got it when the maître d' explained there was no "Great Zambucu." They were maxed out on their credit cards, so they called a friend in the middle of the night to pay their tab. They kept asking the waiter, "If this was a hoax, how did we get in for free?"

Finally, the maître d' brought them a sealed envelope that I had given Gary for this exact moment. The note inside the envelope read:

Ladies, I'm sorry for all the confusion. But maybe, just maybe, there wouldn't have been such a mix-up if you just would have worn your bright red sweaters.

—The Great Zambucu

Now one of the things I've always wondered about myself is why I took such great satisfaction in getting back at these ladies. For me, it doesn't get any better. Over the years, when I tell people this story, it is actually soothing to me. Am I petty and immature? I'm really not sure. But after this happened, I always felt that had I died the next day, I'd have known that justice prevailed.

The Fiber Test

"Hi, Linda, nothing yet, but hang in there."

"Okay, Bruce, you promise you're going to hire me?"

"Of course I'm going to hire you, but I can't fire one cocktail waitress just to hire another. Call me tomorrow."

"I'll come in. I like seeing you. You don't look busy, why don't we talk for a few minutes?"

Wow, I loved hearing that. The only problem, when you are the Food and Beverage Director at a major casino, you cannot get involved with your soon-to-be cocktail waitress.

"Linda, it's going to take all the tricks I know to get the union dispatcher to put you at the head of the list. I hope you understand that."

"Of course I do, I won't let you down, I promise."

"Look, down at the union hall there must be a hundred overweight, middle-aged porkers waiting to be sent out for a cocktail job, and they rarely get hired. What I'm telling you is, at this casino, my employers want gorgeous, sexy, and efficient girls. They could care less about the ladies at the hall and all the dues they've paid."

"Boss, I'm your girl!"

"If you've got a minute, let me tell you a little story."

There were these two gorgeous female lawyers, Debbie and Sue. Both were extremely smart except Debbie got all the guys while Sue never even managed to get a date. Sue, frustrated, finally asked Debbie what was up. Debbie told her friend that her brains intimidated guys and suggested that Sue not act so smart. She needed to go to the brain doctor and have some of her brains removed. Debbie explained to Sue that she'd had it done and her love life couldn't be better now. She told Sue to go see Dr. Smith.

The next day, Sue went to Dr. Smith who put her on the brain machine. The doctor told Sue that he or the nurse would be back in exactly fifteen minutes to disconnect her. Sure enough, both the doctor and the nurse forgot about Sue. Forty-five minutes later they rushed in, quickly disconnected Sue, and started yelling, "Sue, say something, say anything."

Sue looked up, smiled, and calmly said, "Cocktails?"

Linda laughed, missing the point to this story—cocktail waitresses have reputations, so please don't be a flake.

To make this story short, I hired Linda, and for a good month, she epitomized the perfect employee. Then, one night she came to see me in my office.

"Bruce, I know you're going to hate me, but I've taken another job. It's at Wynn's new hotel, and it's going to be the job of a lifetime. Certainly you can't blame me for that."

Was I mad? Damn right! I had pulled a lot of chains to get her hired.

Then Linda made a great point. "Look, I know you went through hell getting me hired and don't think for a minute that I don't appreciate it, but I can't possibly pass up this opportunity. Besides, I know you've got your eye on me and now that you're not my boss, we can go out."

I heard somewhere that the Chinese definition of crisis was "cautious opportunity."

Linda gave me a week's notice, and we set up our first date the night after her first shift at the new job. We went to a quiet little Italian place off the Strip. As I figured, Linda was a lot of fun, the kind of girl who tried like crazy to keep up with my wit but never quite got there. I always love that. I also loved dinner because Linda ordered a bottle of wine and drank it completely. So now, as we headed out the door, Linda asked me what I had in mind for the rest of the evening. I hemmed, hawed, and stammered. Linda said, "Let me tell you what I've got in mind. We'll compare plans and then decide whose is better. How about we stop for one quick drink, then off to your place to test what kind of fiber you're made of?"

"Wow, Linda, you're not going to believe the luck on this

Bruce McGimsey

one. It just so happens that the fiber test is a personal favorite
of mine."

"Oh, come on, Bruce. I know you've never had your fiber
tested by a hot-looking woman like me."

"Au contraire, Linda. You haven't seen any of my moves
yet. Here, let me get the door."

So, off we went. My thinking was that any bar would do,
but oddly enough, she wanted to go to a particular bar. Turn
left, turn left again, down two miles, and turn right. Talk about
being out of the way.

When we finally walked into the bar, ten different people
greeted her. She might as well have been named Norm.
Everyone in the tavern knew her. I headed for a table in the
corner and pulled the chair out for her, only to turn around
and see her at the bar, hugging the bartender. So here we are
at this dingy little pub, exchanging pleasantries with Vinnie
the bartender. Linda pulls out a hundred-dollar bill and starts
playing a poker machine. "Bruce, I'm just going to play a roll.
I promise."

About two hours later, she'd squandered at least a good
two hundred dollars. But that didn't mean she was quitting
so we could finally head back to my place. No, no, now she
borrowed a C-note from Vinnie. I surmised that Linda owed
him more than a hundred dollars, which didn't seem to matter
to him. This in turn made me understand why we went out of
our way to get to this particular joint.

Anyway, not only were we not leaving, but Linda also kept
urging me to play. I hated poker machines, but I needed to
plot my next move because Vinnie would probably have lent
her money all night. Even with his potbelly and comb-over,
I could tell the bartender hoped for his own fiber test. The
more Linda played, the more she drank, and the more she
drank, the meaner she got. I didn't want to be there all night
watching her lose, but that weasel Vinnie told her a guy buried
$500 in the lucky machine she was playing. She had tied on
to that machine and would battle it until it cried uncle or she
completely ran out of bullets.

So, figuring my options, I could hang out all night until she
finally lost, give her cab fare so I could justify to myself leaving

102

her drunk, or reach into my pocket and start playing. Am I the kind of loser who will cling to the one-in-a-million chance that I'm still going to get her back to my place? Or that she would turn it around, win all her money back, then lose the attitude and become a nice, flirtatious person again? Of course I am! Like with most guys, one-in-a-million is better odds than most nights.

Linda played these machines like a typewriter. She zipped through the games so fast I swear she gave away winners. She always played the maximum amount of coins allowed, insisting that anything less was for suckers. I, on the other hand, played these machines slow and methodically, one coin at a time, chicken pecking with one finger.

This made Linda crazy. Already short-tempered, she started ridiculing my form and technique. So what did I do? I wilted under the pressure, completely wimped out, and started betting the maximum. I played poker machines maybe three times in my life for a grand total of ten dollars. Just when I reached the last of my twenty dollars, HOLY ZAMBUCU! I hit a royal! Not only did I hit a royal, but hit it with the maximum coins wagered.

Now, I knew people who played poker machines for years and never hit a royal. Yet on my fourth try, I won a smooth thousand-dollar jackpot. Life was sweet after all. I told Linda I would buy her out of her loan from the bartender, pay her back the money she lost, tip Vinnie a hundred dollars, and still get her back to my house to start the slow, methodical process of measuring fiber.

Excited? Who wouldn't be? Well, for one, Linda wouldn't be. Oddly enough, she never stopped playing. Instead, she just looked at me and said, "If you want to double your jackpot, just press that button." Unbeknownst to me, she referred to a double-down button. I mean, what did I know about poker machines? As it turned out, any time you won, be it a quarter or a thousand dollars, you had the option of pressing that button and wagering everything you just won on one play. People sometimes made this wager when they'd won a little. Virtually no one does it after hitting a royal. Linda never bothered telling me that. When she asked me again if I wanted to double it, she made it appear like no big deal. I even asked her if it meant automatically winning two thousand dollars instead of one thousand, and she said, "Of course, it's easy, just press that button."

Now, being a smart young man with impeccable college credentials from Weber State University, I got to thinking. What's better, two thousand dollars or one thousand dollars? Hmm, two thousand dollars or one thousand dollars? I had no idea that pressing that double-down button still meant gambling. Come on now, what idiot gambles a sure thousand on a one-time roll? Plus the way Linda and Vinnie egged me on, certainly they were looking out for my best interests.

No sooner did I press that button, Linda let out, "You imbecile, do you know what you just did? You gambled a thousand dollars on one roll!" She took such delight. Instead of being happy for me and for us, she laughed and belittled me. The sour, envious look and the bitter tone in her voice were followed by a stream of mocking, sarcastic insults. Linda stewed with jealousy because a rookie hit a royal while she lost three hundred dollars.

I found out later this was a disease known as poker machine envy, a sickness that permeated Las Vegas. Every poker machine junkie in town suffered from the affliction. How many times had this mental disorder cost a deserving man a fiber test? Who knows? I needed to concern myself with the double-down bet.

Once you pressed the deal button, the machine dealt two cards ranging from Ace to King. Then it distributed a third card. If the third card's value landed between the first two, you won. If that third card matched or fell outside the first two cards, you lost. In neighborhood poker games, you called it in-between, acey-deucey, or high-low split.

I figured the odds had to be against me. So when I got dealt two aces, I thought all was lost. But the bartender explained to me that the only way I could lose was to hit another ace. Sadly enough, as the machine dealt out the card, Linda yelled out "Ace!" hoping like hell for me to bust out.

No way! I hit a nine as my in-between card.

Now, somebody out there, please say, "Praise the Lord!"

I won two thousand and literally danced on the bar while I mocked Linda.

"Come on, Linda, give me an amen. Can I please hear one amen while I show off my two-step?"

"Bruce, shove it!"

I finished my jig and my gloating. I gave Vinnie the one-finger salute, bid Linda good riddance, and left her to make it home on her own.

Out in my car, I took a deep breath and reflected on the night. Yeah, I missed out on the fiber test, but I won two grand, stiffed old Vinnie, and got to gloat about it, which all in all amounted to a more lasting memory.

Most important, though, I had broken one of the top three ironclad rules to surviving Las Vegas and lived to tell about it. Don't date cocktail waitresses.

Did that Really Happen?

I've tried to capture on paper some of the casino stories I thought most interesting. These are stories not typical everyday events, but I know they happened and can personally vouch for them. At the same time, occasionally they're also a little bit beyond belief.

Color this one completely strange. It happened to my bar manager, Dexter, in the mid-eighties. One night Dexter called me and wanted me to drop by his office. Long about 7:30 p.m., everything slowed up and I meandered downstairs. Dexter's office sat in the basement of the hotel in a room where we kept the liquor.

As I walked in the door, Dexter offered me a thousand dollars in hundred-dollar bills. "Sit down and wait till you hear this." About 6 p.m. on Tuesday, three nights earlier, Dexter got a call from Hilde, a sixty (going on eighty-five)-year-old cocktail waitress. She'd worked at this casino for thirty-five years, and the last twenty of them in the 21 pit. She made a lot of tax-free money.

Our problem with Hilde stemmed from a lack of hustle. During the course of her shift, the younger girls served almost twice as many drinks. The pit bosses rode Hilde constantly, simply because she was no longer young and pretty. The pit guys wanted sexy young servers so they could try out their tired, stale, New York lines which never worked. Nonetheless, if you worked under the union umbrella, nothing could be done about your age, looks, or quality of service. I understood and related to that rule. At first, young and pretty always took precedent over efficient and competent, no matter what

107

cost to service. But the more I worked my job, the more I looked for balance. Anyway, by the end of her shift, Hilde had received so much abuse that her nerves were shot and she fluttered around like a tattered moth. Over the phone, she yells at Dexter, "The pit needs cigarettes and these assholes are driving me crazy!" In those days, casinos supplied pit players with cigarettes. We kept them in cases of 100. The unenforced rule allowed players to smoke as many as they liked as long as they took them one at a time. Like all the casinos up and down the Strip, we ended the cigarette courtesy years ago, but back then, we stored the cigarettes in the old coatroom.

The coatroom was situated next to the main bar and adjacent to the 21 pit. It was always locked, and by rights, the only departments carrying keys would be beverage and security. Security kept a key to every lock in the building, and once a week housekeeping vacuumed the room under security's supervision. The bar manager maintained the cigarettes.

After Hilde's curt request, Dexter told her to meet him at the cigarette room in five minutes. When Dexter got there, he unlocked the door, and he and Hilde walked in only to find a set of neatly folded clothes sitting on a stack chair in the middle of the room. A sport coat hung over the chair's backrest, and a shirt, pair of pants, and underwear were folded neatly on the seat, with socks tucked into a pair of loafers under the chair.

"What the hell is this?" asked Dexter.

Hilde, in her usual panic, didn't care to know. She grabbed the cigarettes she needed, showed Dexter how many she took, and hightailed it back to the 21 pit.

Dexter, on the other hand, shut the door behind Hilde and decided the circumstances warranted investigation. His first thought, and later on mine, was that one of our cocktail waitresses needed some extra Christmas money. In those days, if a player propositioned a cocktail waitress, she might succumb for the right money. Supposedly frowned upon, it happened all the time anyway. We certainly employed a few girls with, shall we say, an entrepreneurial flair. But there were no closets or curtains in the room. This guy couldn't be walking around the casino without any clothes on.

More mysterious, Dexter found forty-five hundred dollars worth of casino chips in the coat pocket. The wallet in the pants pocket held four thousand dollars in hundred-dollar bills. He also found some credit cards and a driver's license that he didn't recognize. Then again, why would he? Food and beverage people rarely dealt with casino players.

Okay, what to do? Dexter left everything there just the way he found it. He decided to leave the building, go for a drive, and think things over. He ended up calling his wife to get her levelheaded opinion and sagely considered advice.

She said, "What, are you crazy? Go back and take it all."

In those years, the casinos accepted each other's chips. As long as you cashed them in a few at a time, there would be no questions asked. If you tried to cash in a lot of them, the casino called the hotel of origin to see if anyone had won that kind of money. If not, you had some explaining to do.

Dexter made up his mind to go back and finish his shift, and then along about one a.m., slither back to the coatroom. If everything was still just the way he found it, he'd take the money, the chips, and the wallet. Like clockwork, that's just what happened. He dumped the wallet and its contents in a dumpster, less the four thousand in hundreds. He kept the chips, but left the clothes just as he found them.

Dexter usually gave the pit their cigarette fill every other night, unless of course it needed an emergency fill. So he made a point not to go back in there until his required cigarette fill two nights later. When he walked into the coatroom, the clothes were gone and the chair was placed in the corner as if it belonged there. Since housekeeping vacuumed once a week, he surmised they turned the clothes over to lost and found. From there, security absconded with anything of value not claimed, and the rest went to charity. Security's problem then, and still, is they don't get many perks.

So Dexter reasoned take the money or security ends up with it. At least that's how he justified it in his mind. Of course, that's how I justified it too when Dexter offered me the money and explained where it came from. Dexter figured that since there were variables involved he knew nothing about, better to get me involved, so if something came up about this situation, I could possibly cover for him. Besides, he knew I'd enjoy security not getting a dime.

I turned down the money and second-guessed myself for weeks. Hilde never mentioned the incident and probably never gave it a second thought. Thus, thanks to Dexter's initiative and guts, he earned himself a great bonus that night. The only thing that ever gave us pause happened many years later.

Dexter called me one night and told me to turn on the television to this cold case documentary cable show. It recounted an incident that happened at our hotel probably twenty years earlier. A customer mysteriously disappeared not only from our hotel, but also off the face of the earth. The guy never even checked out. He just turned up missing. Dexter had no idea if the clothes he saw that night in the cigarette room belonged to the missing man. It had been too long ago for us to figure if the timeframe coincided. It's just one of those curious Las Vegas stories that will always keep me wondering.

Las Vegas Means Money

Here you have one of the richest men in the world, a man who loves to gamble, lodging at your hotel and casino. Of course, you roll out the red carpet, especially if the guy has a reputation that will fire things up. Add that he's also a huge tipper—or a "George," as we called it. Now, this super high roller stayed in one of the city's oldest and most renowned hotel casinos in Las Vegas. This same casino added what it hoped would be a world-class restaurant to attract big gamblers. They searched all over Europe and the US for the right chef and the right maître d' to impress high rollers like this particular man.

"Hi Bruce, how's it going tonight."

"Oh, thank you very much," I said as he slips a hundred-dollar bill into my shirt pocket. "What are you in the mood for?"

"I feel like some sweet and sour," the millionaire says, "but the pit guy gave me a comp to your fancy new joint."

"Well, you know you can eat wherever you want. Let me seat you here and we'll rustle up that sweet and sour."

"No, let me go up there and check out this new restaurant, and I'll have them send up the food from your coffee shop."

I hated this idea but agreed to it. As the new coffee shop manager of this upscale casino, I had to take a demotion in title, but I made $30,000 a year more in salary. Plus, it was an elite corporation which figured to give me a shot at becoming a director at one of their other glamorous hotels in Vegas or elsewhere around the country. Nonetheless, I didn't get many tips, and I'm thinking I could probably weasel another hundred out of him before he left. Besides, my waitress and busboy

111

were guaranteed to catch a hundred each from this guy. Since I hadn't met the new maître d', this gave me a chance to give him a heads-up on one of the biggest gamblers in the world.

"Yeah, Andre? This is Bruce, manager of the coffee shop. I'm sending you a big shot. He's gonna want some sweet and sour pork so let me know when you want it. By the way, he tips a hundred bucks to just about everybody he talks to."

"Oh, you're going to send him to me? The pit just called me and told me all about him. I'll take it from here."

"Hey, just trying to offer up some help, this guy is important."

"You stick to your coffee shop and I'll be the maître d', okay?"

So now the restaurant buzzed about hoping to make an impression on this guy, and immediately the maître d' hovered all over him. Imagine his surprise when the big shot asked him for sweet and sour pork, just like I told him. The only restaurant in the house that offered sweet and sour pork was the casino coffee shop. The gambler knew this, he just figured the maître d' ought to find a way to get him the sweet and sour. By rights, the maître d' needed to order it at the coffee shop, instruct a busboy to pick it up or have my busboy deliver it like I offered, then add a few frills and serve it. Count on at least a guaranteed hundred in it for him and maybe more.

Now, Andre says to Jim the millionaire, "We don't have sweet and sour on the menu, but let me go back and check with our chef." He went back and asked the highfalutin European chef to take care of it. The chef, feeling insulted, told the maître d' to tell the player that they cook coffee shop food in the coffee shop, so why not head for the coffee shop. Now, please understand that all chefs are jackasses. How to be rude, obnoxious, and belittling are all mandatory classes at chef's school.

So the maître d' headed back and said to Jim, "We don't serve coffee shop food, why not try the coffee shop?" The roller said fine and got up, walked to the taxi stand, and set out to find some sweet and sour. The cab driver recommended a casino downtown and guaranteed satisfaction.

End result, the player loved the sweet and sour pork so much he decided to give the casino a little action. Next thing you know, between blackjack and the crap tables, he dropped five million dollars.

Ask yourself if this classy Strip resort got angry that they lost five million dollars to a downtown casino. Does a French hooker shake it in the moonlight? They not only fired the European chef and the maître d', they proceeded to fire every employee in the restaurant. It took the hotel weeks to put together a whole new crew and reopen the place. Upper management asked me why the maître d' didn't just call me and get the food out of the coffee shop. I so enjoyed retelling the story.

This just goes to show you what the numbers mean to these casinos. Was it the busboy's or the waiter's fault that this rich man took his gambling down the road for a night? Well, a few years later, this same millionaire moved his action up the Strip to one of the new mega-resorts—same corporation, just a different hotel. Still filthy rich, still a notoriously great tipper, and of course still a super heavy player. He kept the casinos catering to his every whim. He expected that when he talked, you answered "Yes, sir, and I will take the ugly one, sir."

Now, it just so happened that I had transferred to that very same mega-resort and held the food and beverage position. So one night I received a call from a cocktail waitress whom I previously worked with and had hired at this new resort. Serving cocktails worked out as a great way to make a living, especially for pleasant looking girls who just happened to have a relaxed attitude about virtue—you know, the kind of virtue that Vegas girls notoriously lacked.

Anyway, Nancy, an absolute delight to look at, moved on to this newly opened resort. In the cocktail lottery draw, she landed the number three slot in seniority, meaning she won a swing-shift pit station making big money. Divorced with two kids at twenty-six, life took a turn for the better. She divorced a deadbeat ex who never made good on his child support. She also got saddled with a huge mortgage due to an ill-advised real-estate choice.

So here lies the dilemma she presented me one early morning about 2 a.m. This same multimillionaire gambler made her a very enticing offer. Simply put, come to his suite when she clocked out at 3 a.m., spend the night, and he would give her one hundred thousand dollars.

She knew this offense might get her terminated. The first idea I came up with, why not get another room at a different hotel? Apparently, this guy couldn't be bothered with that. The offer stood, take it or leave it. My next thought: I suggested she talk to one of the floor men in the pit and feel him out about whether a termination applied. This became her first plan.

An hour later, she called back saying the floor man she addressed took it to the casino manager. The casino manager, through the floor man, told her what she did with her free time was her business. But at the same time, the floor man told her that the hotel appreciated happy players. If she decided not to consent, the relationship between her and the casino might get a little tense. In essence, the casino would gladly pimp out an employee to make a customer happy. They never told her that her actions might jeopardize her job, they just implied it, which now leads to hotel security.

Security policy varies from hotel to hotel. Some never allow solicitation or prostitution whatsoever. Most hotels allow it if the girls minimize their brazen antics—meaning refrain from wearing clothing so offensive and risqué that people stared. A lot of casinos allow it but not at the bars. So your standard prostitute dressed like a tourist, played the slot machines, but still solicited her johns, just in a roundabout way.

A lot of the hotel security force allowed anything as long as they got their taste, meaning pay them off and do whatever you like. The final decision would be in security's hands, and I would have no say in the matter, although the casino manager would have the authority to intercede. All hotels maintained a sophisticated camera system throughout the hotel. If a person, male or female, ended up on an elevator or walking down any hotel corridor, security knew about it. An employee walking into a big shot's hotel suite needed special permission, and it better go through security. These guys invariably develop the little-general complex. So you better pay off security or at least kiss the ring of the sergeant on duty. If not, you bought yourself a lot of trouble.

That night, Nancy wore a black wig, which turned out to

be totally ineffective. She went up, spent the night, and got paid. Before her next shift, she was fired. The casino blamed security and said it was out of their hands. The player figured Nancy got compensated for her choice, so he never stepped up. I felt like I gave her poor advice, so I got her a job at a different casino. That meant she started at the bottom again, back in the coffee shop. The point then and the point now is that the casino used this girl with no regard.

Food and Beverage –
What a Waste

In the hotel casino business, every employee is a potential thief. Millions of dollars are spent every year hiring people to watch the employees to keep them from stealing or catch them at it. Yet despite all that money, casinos still lose a small fortune to employee graft.

The lion's share of a casino's financial resources goes to live gaming and slots. Both customers and employees devote endless time and energy devising schemes to beat the casinos. Owners and upper management know that employees in some departments, like waiters, bartenders, dishwashers, bellmen, etc., occasionally walk out the door with goodies stuffed down their pants. Drinks and meals might not be rung up, and the cash ends up in an employee's pocket. But the cost of controlling this thievery and the hassle of fighting the unions, as they impose their unbeatable rules, simply was too prohibitive. Or so the owners thought.

Occasionally over the years, I or someone else on our food and beverage team caught a cook with product in their pockets or steaks taped to their legs. If we posted someone to watch the dumpsters, we might catch a dishwasher or busboy stashing items out on the trash platform, where they would pick up their ill-gotten goods at shift's end. Casinos also relied heavily on spotters, who worked for a private detective agency completely separate from the casino. The agency in turn hired obscure and sometimes downright weird looking people to pose as customers. They ordered food, drinks, wine, and even played the slots at the bar. They might come in small

117

groups or as singles, and their purchases made it easy for an employee, if so inclined, to steal. The spotters kept track of what they bought and wrote up their findings in a report. The thefts needed to be proven and hold up under union scrutiny. Over a period of ten years, I probably fired at least a dozen food servers and a dozen bartenders because of spotters. All the terminations held up as justified.

I'm sure I barely scratched the surface. My lawyer brother became very popular amongst the crew that worked for me. He held the reputation of being fair and reasonable. I never blinked an eye when one particular bartender went to see my brother to handle a divorce. We investigated this bartender at least three or four times and he turned up with clean spotter reports every time. But during his court hearing, his soon-to-be ex disputed his yearly income, saying that he never claimed any of the cash he stole. Her claim was deemed worthless since she hadn't any proof, but it certainly raised a red flag.

Now the spotters worked him harder, and on their third try, we nabbed him. He always tried to ring drinks in bunches, making it hard to figure how many drinks he actually rang. He'd collect and reuse old receipts that normally should have been thrown away. By rights, a bartender tears the receipt and drops it in front of the customer, so when this guy reused it, he would fake tearing the old receipt in a way that it looked like he had just torn an original. He mastered this move. It took me a dozen tries to spot it on the video tape, and I was looking for it. With the tip his ex gave us, he must have known something smelled. He later told me that the added expensed of his divorce and alimony set him back too much. He needed to keep stealing.

One time, walking through the casino next door, I saw an old buddy I hadn't seen since high school. Steve dealt craps. I went up to the table and said, "Steve, how have you been?" There were no customers at the table, and we'd been good friends in school, but he just stood there looking straight ahead. Now in these casinos, if a table lost a lot of money, sometimes the bosses told you no more talking as a form of punishment. That's how I figured it with Steve, so I told him I'd see him later and headed for the coffee shop. Steve just gave me a look and frowned.

About five minutes later, Steve walked up to me as he headed for his break. He smiled and shook my hand. "Listen, sorry about the cold shoulder, but I couldn't talk to you because I had a hundred-dollar chip in my mouth."

"No kidding? How did you do that?"

"I palm a chip, fake a cough, and cover my mouth. Maybe two, three times a day."

"Do other dealers make the same move?"

"I really don't know, we leave those conversations off the table."

Years later, when I ran into Steve at a high school reunion, I asked him, "Do you still push chips, or have you moved up to management?"

"Hell, no, I couldn't afford management."

Still, the real thievery happened in management, and usually involved more than one employee in on the scheme. A lot of it centered on comps—the complimentary vouchers handed out for food, beverage, show reservations, etc. The gaming bosses divvied out these comps because their job included keeping high rollers happy. Casinos rated a boss's performance on the bottom line gambling figures. The last thing one of these guys needed was to insult a player by not comping him. So writing comps for players figures to be a large part of the casino business. They tracked how much action a player gave the casino and then dealt out the comps accordingly.

The food and beverage director, restaurant manager, bar manager, hotel manager, security chief, etc., also had comp privileges. They generally only wrote a comp in cases of customer dissatisfaction, meaning cold food, poor service, untidy hotel room, slow valet parking, and situations of that nature. Generally, the lower your rank on the management ladder, the lower your comp privileges. For sure, upper management frowned on using comp privileges to play the big shot, like comping your friends or trading your comps with management at other hotels for favors. Of course, that's exactly what we all did. Consequently, you never paid for a meal, a show, or a room at another casino.

Casinos applied only one comping rule to players: try not to waste. If you ordered an expensive bottle of champagne, at least drink some of it. If you got a dinner comp for four and only two of you ate, don't order two extra meals. This was exactly how employees took advantage of the system. If a comp party came in for four but only two people ate, say for a total of twenty dollars, the food server stashed the comp in his pocket and paid the twenty dollars himself. He then waits for a large bill of four worth maybe a hundred dollars. Now he pulls out that stashed comp, uses it to pay the check, and pockets the hundred dollars for a slick eighty-buck profit. Sometimes he might flag the hostess or the cashier to be on the lookout for an expensive bill with four people on it. This was no problem as long as the accomplice got her ten percent. A smart food server even tipped the cooks. That way, she got food without writing it down, enabling her to sell it on her own. This went on at every bar, restaurant, showroom, room service kitchen, whatever. Hundreds of comps got written every month and if a patron failed to use it to its full capacity, an employee stepped up and pounced.

A sharp auditing department should have picked up on this, or least picked up on a missing check where a food server or a cashier just pocketed the money and tore up the check. But auditing always felt overworked and never wanted to bother. They said the department heads should audit their own departments.

The chain of corruption never stops with just auditing. Bar managers, maitre d's, room service managers, banquet bosses and the like would all kick up money to the food and beverage director. If the managers refused, investigations started happening in their areas, and if employees got caught stealing, then restaurant managers got fired for lack of control. Most of the graft took place under the comp umbrella. So the food and beverage statistics, food cost, beverage cost, etc. never fluctuated. The casino just received a lot more comp revenue that actually amounted to nothing. But this enabled the bean counters to balance the books and tell them where the money got spent. Since this corruption went on for so long, the casino owners never knew any better. The comp figures, compared to the cash figures, were a mere pittance compared to bottom line gaming figures. Whenever the owners got wind of the fact that employees ripped them off, they wanted blood. But as long as these scams remained secret, the owners remained blissfully clueless.

A great example happened when we first put a point-of-sale computer system into the beverage department. It was brand-new throughout Las Vegas and intimidated the bartenders because they weren't sure what management could surmise. We naturally led them and the cocktail waitresses to think that we gleaned a lot more information from these computers than possible. They thought the casino ran all comps through the computers and auditing ran a daily audit through the master computer. Sure enough, the first month, the beverage department rang up fifty thousand dollars less in comps and fifty thousand more in cash and credit. This meant in real money, we added fifty thousand dollars a month to the bottom line. On the restaurant side, the figure reached a hundred thousand dollars a month. Did this mean we completely stopped the thievery? Hardly. It just meant we plugged one very large leak.

In my longest food and beverage job, we never ran less than sixty-five percent food cost until I got the head job. In a perfect world, the food cost we strived for in most of our eating establishments was thirty percent—meaning what we paid for the food was thirty percent of what we sold it for. Steak houses did better, but in our coffee shop, which by far did the most business, we ran low-end steak and prime rib deals. By low-end I don't mean inferior meat quality, just that we priced these specials so low that we couldn't run at thirty percent. The same situation applied in our buffet. But with a big room service business, which ran at fifteen percent, and a huge banquet business at the same cost, things should have evened out some. Unfortunately, not so, simply because our chef, our purchasing agent, the sanitation supervisor, and the receiving clerk all stole, stole, stole.

The scams my chef dreamed up were the most ingenious. The food throughout the building tasted great, and the casino owners cared a lot about food quality. They just never realized

Bruce McGimsey

that sixty-five percent food cost penciled out way too high, and none of us dared tell them. Why would we? That kind of stupidly figured to bring us a lot of unnecessary heat and probably get us fired. If the owners knew how badly they were getting beat, heads would have rolled. During the first eight years of the chef's tenure, rumors about the mob owning the hotel held stealing to a minimum, because who wanted to mess with those guys? When the new owners bought the mob out, the chef and everyone else made their move.

By rights, chefs answer to the food and beverage director. But oftentimes, the owners will take jurisdiction over the chef, thus allowing them to play big shot while eating in their restaurants. Bottom line, the chef ended up getting carte blanche.

This exactly described the situation at my joint. Providing the food tasted good, the chef did as he pleased. Our chef did all his own food ordering. He or one of his right-hand men received or checked in all the food orders, and then once a month, he took his own inventory. Now, way back in restaurant management 101, you learn that one person does the ordering, a separate department does the receiving, and accounting should do the inventory. That way, three different people have to collude to steal. As long as they worked in separate departments, it kept managers from threatening an employee for not cooperating because the manager wasn't his or her direct supervisor.

My chef dreamed up scams that took me years to uncover and figure out solutions for. Yet other scams seemed so simplistic that to this day, I kick myself for not seeing through them. I think his best one must have been the meat company scam.

In Las Vegas, casino food outlets all instituted a rule that the purchasing agents needed three separate bids from different meat purveyors every week, always opting for the lowest. Dozens of meat companies existed in the Vegas area, so by rights, a good purchaser kept all of these companies in play. But seeing or calling dozens of purveyors to get a price that rarely differed by more than ten cents a pound took a lot of work. Since the chef did his own ordering anyway, I never questioned seeing receipts from the same three meat

122

purveyors month after month. Nor did I question seeing only one meat representative in the chef's office week after week. But every time I went to accounting, there would always be three separate bids filed on the meat purchase, and one bid always stood out as the lowest. The odd thing was that out of dozens of meat companies, we always got bids from the same three, and during the course of the year, the three companies' orders divided almost equally.

So one day I called one of the companies and represented myself as an assistant food and beverage director from a different hotel. A nice lady named Rose gave me meat prices for a fictitious bid. Rose's hard-line questioning about who I was and my chef's name and so forth made me curious. What did she care, and why grill a potential customer? I didn't really know what to look for, but this seemed just flat out odd.

An hour later, I called the second of the three meat distributors. A gal named Katie answered, and I started getting prices on the same bogus bid. While on the phone, I swore that I recognized Rose's voice in the background, but this couldn't be—she worked at a different meat company. Or did she? I asked Katie her address and she gave me a P.O. box. In fact, all three companies listed different phone numbers, but none of the companies told me where they were located. Okay, different addresses, different phone numbers, but seemingly the same order takers.

It took me a couple of weeks, but I finally found the place. It sat two stores down from where all their meat got stored. It turned out that the three different meat purveyors were actually one company with three separate phone numbers. The meat company owner set up this little charade to do business with dishonest chefs.

He charged thirty to fifty cents a pound higher than market price. Since he controlled the bids of the three phony companies, he just made sure that one bid priced out lower than the other two. If the casino never called any legitimate meat purveyors, only the three bogus ones, how would they know the prices were too high? Thus, once a week, the dishonest meat owner showed up at the casino with the chef's share of the loot.

Even more diabolical, the chef used a special USDA stamper.

Bruce McGimsey

By law, all delivered meat needed to be stamped USDA prime, USDA choice, etc. No-roll meat, meaning ungraded and unstamped, we used as specials—steak and lobster for eight dollars, or steak and eggs for three ninety-nine. When you see prices like these, you better not expect prime beef. But when you visit the Blue Room or the Bacchanal Room and pay seventy dollars for a cut of beef, you certainly expect prime. So when a meat company delivers beef to a restaurant, what ensures a restaurant that it's getting the quality and grade it ordered? By rights, everything gets stamped. But with a lot of our cuts, the stamps were not legible. They appeared blurred, apparently from bleeding, so you couldn't quite tell what grade the meat was. As it turned out, the meat company possessed a special stamp that intentionally printed a blurred marking. Therefore, the company delivered choice instead of prime but got away with charging prime prices. If an inspector showed up, the chef always left a small pallet of beef thawed just enough to let the ink run. A foolproof scam like this amounted to as much as eighty cents to a dollar a pound.

The easiest move the chef used came with product delivery. Like most casinos, we utilized our own in-house bakery as much as possible, but every other day we took delivery of hundreds of specialty dessert pieces for our fine dining room. These extra-rich cakes and pastries arrived in racks or sheet pans. One afternoon, while in detective mode, I saw these desserts being delivered to our bakery. The assistant baker in charge of taking delivery never bothered to count them, he just signed off on them. I asked him why, and he said the chef told him not to bother because it took too much time. Sure enough, we counted. It turned out the specialty house charged for eight hundred pieces but only delivered six hundred. This amounted to a real chunk of money that the chef cut up with this bakery. Was he doing this with every purveyor we did business with? Probably. The worst thing about this scenario, other bandits still needed to be dealt with.

The next great thief turned out to be the purchasing agent. Simply put, a good purchasing agent buys the best quality for the least amount of money, but in some instances it's okay if quality takes a back seat to price to perk up some bottom line percentages. First, an agent goes about receiving bids from purveyors, usually through sales reps who come by weekly. Eventually, a good rep gets the purchaser to quit seeing the competition. Instead of receiving multiple bids on each purchase, the agent receives one. The rep's next step is to bring in gifts, until finally, the gifts are replaced with cash. Now he pretty much owns the purchasing agent so he can charge inflated prices without any complaints.

My purchasing agent came off as particularly arrogant. He happened to be the owner's brother and apparently was a sacred cow. I remember a china salesman coming to me with an offer on china that substantially beat the price of our current offer, yet he never got through our purchasing agent's door to offer his bid. So I took his bid and presented it to our purchaser, Dale. Dale, of course, trotted out his standard pitch, that the quality lacked. He tossed out a lot of fancy terms and eventually sent me packing. "Since I've been doing this for years," he said, "I know all the tricks that rookies fall for. Just stick to food and beverage and let the experienced people worry about the bottom line."

I asked, "Do you think I'm an idiot?"

"No, but you think the same manufacturer made this china and it matches our current china exactly. But I'm telling you it doesn't, and the quality is lacking."

"Sure, Dale." This guy maintained his own little business, and I knew it. The problem at this juncture, I was the only one who knew. The other problem, as it turned out, was that I had my own problem.

I worked for this company for eight years, and over those eight years, like it or not, I stepped on toes, and animosities developed. This probably holds true for every corporation in the world. So, in my hotel, you often never really knew your enemies. For instance, if you disciplined a cocktail waitress, did you know for sure whom she slept with last night? Does she flirt with the pit, then suggest that the pit boss ought to complain about overall service to the casino manager? So the casino manager reams you out, never telling you where the complaint came from, leaving you clueless. You're not even sure if the complaint warrants your attention. Or maybe you uncover a food server stealing. If she suspects you're onto her before you drop the hammer, it spells big trouble. She might command the owner's ear or the general manager's, or for that matter, maybe even the casino managers', simply because she waits on them all the time. I might talk to upper management once a month. But the big shots loved to mingle with the common help. It empowered them to feel like they walked in step with the average workers when actually the employees played them.

So what happens? About a year after the hotel promoted me to the position of Food and Beverage Director, they hired a new General Manager who knew nothing about the business. He came from back East with a background in zoo management. We never found out just how many rocks they looked under to find this guy. His incompetence personified stupidity, kind of like a chimpanzee, if I'm not being too tough on the ape.

Now, for the eight years I worked at this place and tried to do the best job I knew how, I never took money from maitre d's or restaurant heads. No one ever bought their job from me, either with money or sex, and anybody I caught stealing, I fired, no matter who they knew. My immediate boss, the guy who mentored me, carried himself the same way. As far as I knew, he also always performed at peak level. He eventually moved to a big-time casino for a lot more money, and they promoted me to his job. Like Gary, I aspired to make it to one of the elite casinos. About the only illicit act we ever committed was overusing our comp privileges, but trust me, everyone in every casino indulges in that.

My troubles derived from two sources. The new GM took idiocy to a new level. I hadn't handled all the graft and corruption going on in my department, only some of it. So when a half-pallet of shrimp turned up missing one night, the new GM surmised I needed firing. He never blamed me for stealing, rather I got blamed for not stopping the stealing. It took the GM, Curly Rocha, a week before he and the new director waited in my office. Even though I sensed a lot of problems with Curly, this still caught me off-guard. The idiot explained to me that I needed a little more seasoning, so he demoted me back to assistant. He said, "Please take the new director and introduce him to management and staff around the building."

Curly planned for me to walk off the job in a huff, figuring me to protest the demotion and refuse to accept the humiliation of introducing the new director to my employees. The imbecile never knew that he could fire me for no reason. Nevada was a right-to-work state, meaning unless you worked under union protection, you could be fired simply for a change in personnel. So I did it because I just shuddered at the prospect of giving in to a simpleton like Curly.

This cornered Curly into plan B, which meant forcing the new director to find a reason to fire me. As it turned out, the new guy loved writing memos. He blew memos out of his computer all day long, keeping the GM informed of his plans. When he first got there, he naturally took the biggest office in our department, which currently sat empty. Officially, it was the Food and Beverage Director's office, I just never used it. Little did this guy know, I had a key. So now, every night when the new director left, I scurried in and searched his office. I read all his notes and memos and also scanned his computer, which gave me a heads-up on how he planned to fire me. Twice I embarrassed him in front of Curly and one time the owner even witnessed it.

At the same time, I finally figured out some of the chef's and purchasing director's schemes. They stole in such big chunks that if corrected, the food cost might go down twenty percent. As information evolved, the shrimp and other missing goodies were the work of the sanitation director. He oversaw sanitation—cleaning kitchens, floors, dishes, etc.—and over the years, he slyly put together a crew of Cubans, matching his heritage. Whenever any of them got a shot at stealing, they threw the booty into a food warmer and walked it slowly through the building. Not to the dumpsters, like I reasoned, but to Santos the sanitation director's office. There, he stored everything from shrimp to boxes of china, silverware, liquor, wine, etc., and moved it out in his truck. He built a false bottom into the bed of his truck, and to help camouflage his stolen goods, he put bags of empty beer and soda cans on top of the contraband. We received so much banquet business that he amassed a never-ending collection of tin cans just waiting to be hauled. He drove through our security check and never got stopped. Anyway, I looked good uncovering all this.

Curly called me into his office and asked me why the new guy appeared to flounder so much. Now I felt the need to make my move. I laid out all the various players and all their plots and scams. I wowed Curly to the point that he was both enthralled and impressed. First thing the next morning, he fired the purchasing agent, who of course happened to be the owner's brother. Then he fired the new director, but instead of reinstalling me, he hired another director, leaving me as the assistant. If he rehired me, it meant explaining to the owner why, which in turn meant giving me the credit for uncovering all the graft going on. Therefore, he would be forced to admit it wasn't his brilliant managerial expertise that created this newfound money.

First rule you learn in management school, don't suppress the creative energy beneath you by not recognizing good ideas. The first month with the new purchasing agent, we lowered our food cost by ten percent. Curly took all the credit with the owner and promised him more. What's more, the newest director, Smiling Jack Applerod, thought he deserved the credit for the lower numbers. Smiling Jack took idiocy to a new level.

Smiling Jack made a lot of mistakes right from the get-go. First off, he set out to fire all the room managers and maitre d's and put in his own people, thus giving the new heads carte blanche to steal any way they deemed possible. His only stipulation was that he wanted ten percent. Since all the current room heads were accustomed to me, he felt the need to get rid of us all. The underlying problem, Jack never recognized his true enemies. The various room heads mastered kissing up to both bosses and owners alike, meaning they commanded a lot of respect.

For his second move, to impress Curly, he decided to hire a food and beverage consulting firm. The consulting team came in for a couple of weeks and delivered what they hoped would become a monthly report on how to lower the food cost and improve employee efficiency. Most of their ideas seemed valid, but at best penny-ante suggestions that might move the numbers a percentage point. So when Curly asked me about the numbers, I explained it just that way. He questioned if their fee really equaled better bottom line numbers. Besides, Curly had yet to lower the boom on the chef, the sanitation director, and the warehouse receiving clerk. As he checked out the information I gave him, one percentage point looked like peanuts in comparison to the twenty percentage points I promised him.

Jack's third mistake was trying to fire me. Long about the second month of Jack's tenure, the numbers were still down ten percent simply because we hired an honest purchasing agent. Yet Jack, in all his department head meetings, kept trying to take credit for the lower food cost. This aggravated the hell out of Curly. After all, Curly already cornered all of that credit. So now, the consulting team told Jack they knew of a perfect replacement for me. She worked for an Atlantic City casino. Jack, a blithering idiot in his own right, never bothered to consult Curly about this. He okayed it through Mike, the hotel manager, who by rights Jack reported to. Mike's fancy job title never matched his authority, he just didn't know it. Together, the two of them brought Cindy out from Atlantic City. They set her up with a hotel room for as long as necessary. She showed up on a Saturday, which set my termination for Monday.

Bright and early Monday morning, Jack and Mike decided to inform Curly. I already sniffed this out and had asked Curly about my getting fired. He told me no and that he'd take care of the whole situation. Curly knew that firing me made no sense because someone led him to believe there might be some more in-house scams. Thus Curly told Jack and Mike that Cindy was not only not hired, he wanted her out of the hotel room that day. He also told Jack to get rid of the consulting agency.

By far the biggest mistake Jack ever made was never changing the lock to his office. So again, I knew every move he made ahead of time. I not only knew of my pending termination, I also knew the consulting company offered him a kickback for his cooperation. I knew Cindy offered him $500 for her job, and when she left that Monday, neither Jack nor Mike helped her move. Since I owned a truck, I volunteered. She told me about not only the $500, but also a friend of hers whom Jack hired in our fine dining room who gave Jack ten percent of his tips. Knowing Jack's character, I figured maybe if the detective agency spotted the new waiter, we might just catch a thief red-handed. Not only did I catch him, but he rolled over on Jack and helped me set him up.

That ended Smiling Jack Applerod. Within two months, Curly let the hammer drop on the chef, Santos, and the receiving clerk. Four co-managers finally got caught stealing too. So in a year's time, I saw more just deserts than most people see in a lifetime. Over the years, who knows how many food guys lost their jobs because of bad bottom line numbers due to managers from other departments who stole. On top of that, I got two of my immediate superiors fired before they fired me. How sweet was that?

I worked at this casino for another year. Our food cost came in consistently between 32 and 35 percent, for which Curly took all the credit, of course. At year's end, I got in a beef with the culinary union. They threatened to go to the labor relations board if the casino refused to fire me. The union wanted me out because of my popularity with the casino's union employees. The union wanted no part of management that might sway union membership. With a potential strike in the works, who needed someone on the other side presenting a logical viewpoint contrary to theirs? So they brought in outside witnesses to say I broke negotiation rules set up by the National Labor Relations Board. Curly decided, cheaper to fire me than stand up and fight. I understood that, and would have accepted it, just like I understood the union's underhanded actions and accepted them. But Curly made up other reasons, figuring I wouldn't find out the truth. It took about two days before someone in the union laid it all out for me.

Okay then, what to do? I felt that after all I gave that company and measuring the amount of money I saved them, they owed me the truth. My first thought, maybe corner Curly in the hallway and give him a piece of my mind. That seemed empty and unsatisfying. Maybe the standard high school stuff where you follow him home and slice his tires? No way, too childish, besides, he lived at the hotel and valet handled his car. I just felt that I wanted to see a little more justice.

Then it hit me! Curly moved into the hotel about six months after he got the job. He always said that he never accepted a raise, figuring that justified his never giving us a raise. But he did get a raise. He and his wife lived at the hotel for free, at least for two years. They gave his wife a bogus little job with a bogus title so she also earned a paycheck. I bet that neither one of them reported free living accommodations to the IRS.

It just so happened that I went to college in Ogden, Utah, regional home of the IRS. I had a friend who worked for the IRS in middle management. Not only could I get them audited, but if the audit proved successful, as a reward, I'd receive a percentage of what they owed. A simple call to Ava, my buddy in the payroll office, and I knew both of their Social Security numbers. Off I went. As it turned out, besides living in a hotel suite, they relied on the hotel to do all their cleaning and feed them, and they used a hotel car for transportation. Gotcha!

The Lord Works
in Mysterious Ways

I had met Gineel my last year of college. An aspiring nurse, Gineel owned me right from the start. It took her approximately one year to jilt me for a real retard, whom we'll call loser number one. Brokenhearted, I moved back to Vegas and started my push to be a millionaire. I never quite got Gineel out of my system, though, and eventually made my way back to Salt Lake City to rekindle the flame. As it happened, loser number one had left long ago and she had just divorced loser number two. We picked up where we left off until a year later. You guessed it, she dumped me for loser number three. So, I moved back to Las Vegas.

A pattern certainly had developed. About a year later, Gineel looked me up. Gone was loser number three, and fresh on the scene arrived loser number four, me. Sure enough, I moved out of Las Vegas back to SLC to give Gineel one more chance. Do I need to define stupid here?

Our romance lasted a good three years. Her parents were staunch Mormons, which always made me nervous. Whenever we went to their house for dinner, Gineel asked me not to be weird. She'd say, "Can you make it that long? If they ask you a question, try to think how a human would respond." She, of course, fancied herself a clever girl, but it stuck in my craw. She told me she needed this type of fantasy to help her justify me to her family and friends. At this time, she loved the show "Mork and Mindy" and truly believed I came from a different world.

Long story longer, Christmas day rolled up, and we planned to go to Gineel's parents' house to exchange gifts. Since she

133

Bruce McGimsey

always led me to believe that her parents thought I was the weirdest thing since Jimmy Swaggert, this made me nervous. I psyched myself up—okay, a half-hour visit, trade Christmas pleasantries with the family, then out the door for more comfortable circumstances. Gineel, on the other hand, thought her boyfriend should know enough to want to spend the entire Christmas day with the girl he loved. We argued, I left, and that ended Gineel and me.

Within a month, she replaced me with the biggest loser of her life. Six months later, she called me on my birthday to tell me she got married, undoubtedly to another loser, but since it might take a while to know for sure, I placed him in the loser pending file.

For the next twelve years, I never saw Gineel. You know, out of my life, but not quite out of my mind. During this period I got married and divorced, went through three or four girlfriends, but only once came close to replacing Gineel, meaning Sheila. I'm talking about a great girl with our only real problem being that I still wouldn't let Gineel go. By this time, I harbored no delusions about her feelings for me, and I figured she rarely thought about me, if ever.

Now keep in mind, we knew each other seven years. Her parents grew up old-fashioned and expected our courtship to run along old-fashioned parameters, like asking her father for permission to wed their daughter and things like that. Well, in seven years never once was there any mention of a dowry. Do you call that old school? Me neither. Between her parents and her ridicule on Christmas Day, I really started to wonder who turned out being the loser. I had heard she lived in Phoenix with three kids. So one fateful day, when I'd briefly returned to Salt Lake for business, I decided to cruise by her parents' house just like a high school kid.

Gineel's parents lived in the same house throughout their adult married lives. The outside of the house changed a bit, but the house's surroundings changed a lot. No longer did the house sit off by itself. Other houses now surrounded theirs on three sides and a four-story apartment complex sat directly behind it. So picture an apartment complex, a parking lot full of cars, and then on the front right corner of the parking lot, Gineel's parents' red brick house. It had a huge backyard enclosed by a six-foot-high wire fence. Somewhere along the line, they'd planted ivy along the fence, obviously to obtain some semblance of privacy. It looked as if the third and fourth-floor apartment balconies commanded a perfect view of both their backyard and the big picture window to their dining room. Nonetheless, at eye level, the greenery enshrining the fence seemed very thick.

I pulled into the parking lot next to their house and sat in my car, laughing to myself as to how childish this was, when what do you know, I see an old college friend. I waved him over.

"Bruce, haven't seen you in years, what are ya doing?"

"Oh, nothing really. I live in Vegas and came up here to fix up my condo so I can sell it. You?"

"Sales rep for a national outfit, brass fixtures and hardware." Doug pointed up at the apartment building. "My wife and I live up on the fourth floor, that's our balcony. Hey, didn't your old girlfriend live in that house? I thought she dumped you."

"More than once."

"And you're gonna go see her again? Are you stupid?"

"I'm trying to make sure I'm not kidding myself about asking my new lady to get married."

"Sounds crazy to me, but do what you got to do, and then come see us, we're in 4110."

I couldn't see through the vines, and I really sensed trouble somehow. Anyway, just as I decided to leave, I heard voices coming from the backyard. So, what's an immature guy to do but get out and investigate? A row of parked cars paralleled their fence with bumpers buttressed against the ivy fence. Now, if a strange forty-year-old man got down on his hands and knees in broad daylight and crawled twenty yards down this fence line between greenery and bumper, he could probably get a load of any action happening in the backyard. Of course, if anyone from the apartments sat out on their balcony, they figured to see this weirdo and wonder what the hell he was doing. No problem.

Sure enough, halfway down the fence line on all fours, I look up towards Doug's balcony and he's standing out there staring at me. I imagine Doug calling out to his wife, "Kelli, come here and look what this idiot Bruce is doing." Next thing I know, his wife is out there looking at me too.

I've got to tell you, accepting the idea that you're a little strange isn't that tough. I'd known it for years. Getting caught being strange is embarrassing, but if you don't know any of the players involved and you know you'll never see them again, you learn to adjust pretty easily. However, when friends catch you being weird, you start imagining them telling everyone you know just how whacked out you are, which makes you sweat and throws off your game.

What can I say? I'd come this far, so friends be damned. I finished crawling to the end of the fence, rose up to my feet, spread the thick green stuff apart, and slyly gawked into their backyard. I saw a volleyball net and two boys and a girl batting a ball around more like soccer than volleyball. Their ages roughly ranged between eight and twelve, obviously grandchildren. Gineel's siblings numbered three brothers and four sisters, so undoubtedly a never-ending supply of grandkids kicked around that house. As I watched the three little dorks rough up the game of volleyball, I noticed a lady standing at the back door. My first thought was this must be Gineel's mother, because she looked so familiar. But, like all kids do, one of the three bozos shouted, "Mom!" and I realized the lady at the door looked a lot like Gineel's mother twenty years earlier. It wasn't pretty. This lady at the door was huge. I'm talking NFL linebacker. I mean no daylight between her and the doorframe. Then someone inside yelled, "Gineel," and the walrus at the door answered back. Forgetting myself, I laughed out loud, then ducked in case someone heard me.

So now I'm crawling down the pathway on my hands and knees and I look up to see my friends in the balcony laughing. I'm just hoping nobody else saw me and called the cops. Any minute now those swirling red and blue lights might light up the lot and the police would haul me away as some kind of sexual deviant. All told, none of it mattered. This girl, who possessed my every thought for years and broke my heart three different times, now looked like an oinker. I giggled, laughed, and slithered back to my car.

First thing I did was head up to Doug's apartment hoping for a little damage control.

"Bruce, what are ya doing?"

"Trying to close the books on my old girlfriend, and as it turns out, she's an oversized cow."

"So, mission accomplished?"

"Are you kidding?" I wiped the imaginary sweat from my brow. "Thank you, Lord."

Doug laughed, but Kelli was giving me the evil eye. I tried to explain. "This bartender who worked for me at the casino, all year long he'd flirt with these gorgeous cocktail waitresses, and then at our Christmas party, he'd bring his fat wife in and introduce her around. Not only was he embarrassed by her, he acted ashamed, and truth of the matter, that would have been me, I'd have been making excuses to leave early every time I ventured out in public with her. Are all guys that superficial, or just me?"

Kelli made a face. "Are you kidding? All guys are like that."

"Gineel was the apple of my eye and the love of my life, she owned my heart and was the closest I came to having a best friend for years. Now you're telling me all guys are that shallow?"

"Hell, yes, at least that shallow."

Now in utter euphoria, I turned to Doug. "Thank you, God, we're all weird."

"Not so fast, Bruce. I wasn't down there sliding around on my belly. You're lucky Kelli didn't call the cops. But once I explained what a nut case you were, she cut you some slack."

"Thank you, Kelli, you've got to understand how big a weight has lifted from my heart. I not only don't desire her, but one look at her has killed any longing for her whatsoever. And the best thing is, I no longer have any ill will about our history. I can finally say I wish her all the best and mean it."

"What about your current girlfriend?"

"That's even better. I feel like giving her a big hug. I wish she was here right now."

"What if you marry her and she gets fat?"

"I'll jump off that bridge when I come to it."

I kept scheming up ways to run into Gineel as a chance

encounter, just to gloat. Was this the normal reaction of a forty-year-old man? In the end, I never devised a plan to accidentally bump into her. Just the fact she carried around an extra sixty-five pounds satisfied me. But I must admit, I almost exploded waiting to relate this story to my best friend, Larry. Sure enough, Larry loved it. He seemed as thrilled as I was, so maybe all guys are that shallow.

I received an epiphany that day. All those years earlier, I carried on a conversation with God, you know, one of those times when you think you're in dire need of a miracle. I said, "Lord, if you will deliver Gineel back into my arms, I vow I will not only become a good person but will stay a good person for the rest of my life."

On that day, the Almighty, in his infinite wisdom, finally answered me. "Bruce, let's get real. You're not capable of being a good person. If you can last just one week doing the good guy thing, then we'll talk." Like always, the Big Guy figured it pretty well.

Superficial – Who, Me?

Women love romance so much, I always called them suckers for love. But I never actually knew that for sure. If a guy developed his game well enough to entice a female simply by his romantic prowess, an average-looking man might occasionally hit the big time. Most guys will always swing for the fences, looks or no looks. But the everlasting question that constantly echoed through my shallow head, are women superficial?

In my lifetime, I had a friend or two who would occasionally say, "Let's go out and meet some women tonight," and actually mean it. I'm talking about men who were good-looking and knew it. Meeting the opposite sex came easy for them. They never stumbled around trying to be clever, they just made sure not to be obnoxious. Be nice, smile a lot, and good things happen.

I, on the other hand, seemed to always smell like a wet dog. To get anywhere, I juggled, did impressions, told funny stories, bought all the drinks, and then maybe got some digits at the end of the night. Of course, the next step was to pray like hell that I'd received a legitimate phone number. Anyway, as one of my all-time fantasies, I wanted great looks so that just once in my life I could be one of the good-looking people, able to walk into a nightclub, turn heads, and see how superficial women were. Would they swoon and be willing to embarrass themselves like so many guys did? Pipedream or not, I felt a never-ending curiosity to answer that very question.

In the years I spent as a self-proclaimed casino big shot, I ran into a has-been movie star eating in the hotel coffee shop.

Bruce McGimsey

He had starred as a child actor in half a dozen movies, but, like so many child actors, his career hit the skids once he grew up. Only in his mid-twenties, he had unfulfilled movie star aspirations, so he still immersed himself in the Hollywood scene. Now, he and a friend sat in the coffee shop while the waitress kept trying to run his maxed-out credit card. "Hey, trust me. I'm a movie star and I'm good for it. Please don't embarrass me like this."

I not only recognized him, I could name a few of his movies. I doubt anyone in the restaurant bought his story, so when I signed for his check, it brought him stature that appeared to relieve his uneasiness. He then asked me to sit down and proceeded to fascinate me with a bunch of Hollywood stories. He showed me a lot of respect and patiently answered all of my weird questions. But for me, his friend seemed more important, or shall I say, what his friend did for a living seemed more important.

As it turned out, my new friends showed up in Vegas about once a month. Never pushy about things, they still notified me when they hit town because they enjoyed my comp privileges, so why not? They never asked for expensive shows or eateries, just the coffee shop or buffet. No problem. I enjoyed their stories, and I had a favor of my own to ask.

The has-been's friend just happened to be a Hollywood makeup artist. He created monsters in horror movies, spending hours turning normal-looking people into creatures. Now I asked him the big question. "Is there any possibility of making an artificial face and turning me into a super-looking man? Like in Mission Impossible, when Tom Cruise takes off his pseudo bad-guy face and reveals himself as the hero. I mean, is that a possibility, or only in the movies?"

"I specialize in outer space creatures," he said. "But yeah, I could do it. What's the purpose?" That's when I explained to these guys my constant dream of being a super-stud one night of my life. He said, "No problem, with one stipulation. I'll make a bust of a twenty-five-year-old friend of ours who happens to be one of the many young leading man wannabes kicking around Hollywood. This guy suits your purposes to a tee. We're talking a lot of work here, but it sounds like fun. So, if we can come with you on this big night out, I'm in."

Since I was in my mid-thirties and these two in their twenties, they insisted on outfitting me in the current fashions. Translation: I dressed like a geek. Also, I think they wanted to make sure that no nefarious motives lurked about, like knocking off a bank. Since this artificial rubber-like mask would take up to four hours to make, I understood their concern. At the time, I weighed in at one hundred eighty pounds, about ten pounds over my fighting weight. Still, as long as I kept my shirt on, my outstanding new face should carry the day. I still had all my hair, but if my shirt came off, real skin meeting phony becomes obvious. I'd be going home alone.

I picked a club frequented almost exclusively by the beautiful people. With my outdated dance moves, my friends warned me to stay off the dance floor. Besides, I needed to avoid sweating so as not to compromise my disguise.

My buddies turned me into handsome personified, just an amazing job. It took me about half an hour to get into character. After all, going from ordinary to gorgeous was no everyday occurrence. Just walking into this place, I received the most incredible looks and smiles. Girls went out of their way to flirt with me, and if I smiled back or winked, watch out. No wonder good-looking people act so conceited. It's unnerving!

I planned to heed my good-looking college friend's advice and just be nice. No one asked me to dance, nor did anyone buy me drinks. No, the women acted a little more coy and subtle than most men did. But everywhere I went inside that club, some lady showed up and started a conversation with me. I tried not to take much notice of the girls who already accompanied guys. After all, I saw no need to get into a fight. Why should I? It seemed every single woman in the place wanted me.

On this night out, most of the girls suggested we get together later on, and if I stalled, they slipped me their number whether I asked for it or not. The girls never got graphic or crude, they just let it be known that they had game.

We avoided asking girls to sit with us for a drink. After

Bruce McGimsey

all, this being a social experiment, I didn't want to tie myself down with the same girl for the whole night. So I table-hopped from one set of girls to another. It truly amazed me how they vied for my attention. In this respect they acted just like guys, meaning that they constantly found reasons to touch me. They either put their hand on my arm or briefly put their arm around my shoulders. Subtle enough, but occasionally it got awkward because I didn't always enjoy the advances. Think how rough it must get for women trying to fend off clumsy come-ons from men, who undoubtedly acted ten times more aggressive and not nearly as subtle. As the advances continued, I even started feeling a little arrogant. You know, that attitude like, "Hey, lady, I can have anybody in this room, what makes you think I'd choose you? So please don't touch me."

The real fun started when I saw a guy I worked with, an assistant chef at my casino. Benny zeroed in on a little princess at the bar. Already married to a nice young woman, he still fancied himself a real lady's man. Most nights, he flew solo. Benny stood about five foot eight and was not a belligerent type, so I figured him for the mask's first real test without worrying about any fisticuffs breaking out.

I rated Benny's girl as pleasant looking but not gorgeous. Nicely shaped, she seemed about twenty-five, with her most distinguishing attribute being her constant beautiful smile. She appeared to love having fun and particularly to laugh.

Since I desperately wanted to test out my new disguise, I confronted the two of them, smiling at her and acknowledging him with a nod. "Listen, I've had my eye on you for a while now, and I just know you can't be with a loser like this."

Now, I expected Benny to at least recognize my voice and blow my cover.

"Do I know you?" he asked in a very combative tone.

"No, buddy. I think better of myself than to associate with lowlifes. I just figured this cutie needed saving from the likes of you." Then I immediately turned my attention to Benny's potential conquest.

I felt like a major league center fielder because she couldn't get enough of me. I asked for her phone number right in front
142

of Benny. She not only gave it to me but also suggested we hang out together. Benny finally limped away like a puppy dog with a hurt paw.

I now understood why I hated good-looking guys so much. They came away as classless, obnoxious creeps. So now I wondered, better to be a Gorgeous George or a Fran Tarkington? Either way there was no justice in this world.

I bled my new circumstances until the ice melted in our last drink. When lo and behold, who do I spot on the dance floor but Lindsay Snow and Suzie Beau. Yes, siree, as I live and breathe. There were the two blind-date ladies from T.G.I. Fridays, slutted out like Parisian streetwalkers. A few years back, on the phone, Lindsey Snow told me she hung out here, so deep down, I kind of hoped to see them tonight. Three or four years had passed since our last encounter, and they clearly leaned on the upper side of thirty-five. Did they belong in a young, trendy joint like this? Who knows? But circumstances certainly warranted investigation.

I walked over and started talking to them. They asked me stuff like, how would you like a home-cooked meal? Are you looking for someone who can bring something to the table? Finally, it dawned on me. These two honestly believed they deserved a shot at a looker like me. What's more, they even seemed to believe beautiful men could make great husbands. What a Walter Mitty world these two lived in.

In case you forgot, these two definitely came from Kansas. What's more, they foolishly imagined they belonged with the trendy people, mingling with us young studs. For a brief instant, I almost felt sorry for them.

So, not wanting to be a mere bimbo, I decided to throw them a little fun, and told Lindsay to call me. Of course, I gave her a bogus number. So what did Lindsay do? Just like an insecure loser, she went out in the hall and called that number. Hell, that's exactly the kind of thing I always did. Next thing I knew, she stormed back onto the floor screaming at me.

"Where do you get off giving me a phony number? What, you think you're so hot that you're giving me a thrill for the night? I didn't ask for your number!"

Bruce McGimsey

Now I just wanted to get her out of my face. Talk about embarrassing. They followed me around like pet gerbils. So, finally, I turned around to face them with the coldest, sternest look I could summon. "Look, why don't you two put on your red sweaters and go find the Great Zambucu?"

Confused, shocked, speechless, this shut Lindsay up long enough for us to escape. Here's the rub. Lindsay's shallow, empty, and unfulfilled desire to find that great-looking man reminded me of someone. Me! I might as well have looked into a mirror. Was this my destiny, to constantly be searching for some plastic, physical, superficial relationship with no depth or purpose? I honestly felt sorry for her, and for the first time in my life, I felt bad for the tricks I played on her years earlier. She figured to be a normal human being working as best she could with the hand dealt to her. Who was I to step on her dreams? But the question I asked myself was, do I have the capacity to learn from this experience? This shaped up to be a pivotal moment in my life so I needed to jump on it and learn something.

Finally that night, thanks to my Hollywood friends and Lindsay, I felt I received another epiphany from above. I vowed, no more sleazy women, and I'd also start looking in better places, like social gatherings, or through friends, and who knows, maybe even church.

Well, I'm here to tell you, that total commitment I made that night had to be the longest seventeen minutes of my life. Just the amount of time it took to get from the club to a high-end topless joint.

Time to face the facts. I'm a superficial guy and I love it.

Just Like Clockwork

Who am I? Where am I going? And how come every woman I meet hates me? Are these questions every forty-plus man asks, or just me? It seemed the women I met always ended our conversations with a proposition that included a price tag. So, as I hovered around the Big Four-Oh, self-doubt and worry dominated my everyday thoughts, affecting my sleep, my work habits, even my golf game. Was I to go through life single, with no children, working a meaningless mid-level management job? I wanted to amount to something, not write warning slips to tardy cocktail waitresses. Had my career peaked? Was I ever going to be a wheel making decisions that enhanced little people's lives, or had I become one of those little people feeding off the scraps of big shots?

I dreamed of a son throwing fastballs past Yankee sluggers. Certainly a fun guy like me owed the world a Bruce Junior. Was I living in a fantasyland? I have to admit I hung on to believing in Santa Claus way past the norm. Hell, for that matter, until just a few years ago, I used to fart in my gas tank every morning believing I could get better mileage. Yup, just like clockwork, I seemed to be knee-deep in a mid-life crisis with no direction except that slow drive to crazy.

What to do? I needed to get on top of this. Like most people, I couldn't keep from comparing my situation to others'. Everyone around me seemed so happy and content. So, with no real plan, I decided to call some friends and find out how they dealt with life. I knew that if they were sailing through their forties without any real problems, it would only shake my world that much more. But, I compiled a list of friends

145

anyway, mostly guys but also a few girls, from childhood, high school, college, golf buddies, co-workers etc. Here is a sample of the most important conversations.

"Hi, Doug, Bruce McGimsey, how you doing?"

"Bruce! Great to hear from you. How's everything?"

"To be honest, I'm depressed. My job is a dead end. I'm single, lonely, I doubt if I'll ever have kids, and all that bothers me."

"Bruce what's the problem? Aren't you in charge of the cocktail waitresses? A different girl every night? Who needs some big fat wife getting in your way?"

"Doug, Doug, Doug, first off, it doesn't work that way. We don't touch our employees or it's big trouble for us, and are you telling me Kelli has gained a few since I last saw you?"

"Hey, a few would be acceptable, even twenty, but hell, last week at the doctor's, he told her to open wide and say oink. Trust me, you need to stick with those cocktail waitresses you say you never touch and be glad you don't have a Kelli who, I guarantee you, you'd never want to touch."

"Mike, it's Bruce McGimsey from college."

"Bruce, I've been meaning to call you. You still have lawyer brothers?"

"Yeah, I do, what's up?"

"Ask them how I can disown my sixteen-year-old son."

"You serious?"

"I hate the little bastard and he's ruining my life! Can you call me back on this tonight?"

"Kenny, Bruce McGimsey, how's it going?"

"Going? I'll tell you how it's going. You still work in a casino down in Vegas?"

"Yeah...?"

"You know a hit man I could hire to kill my wife?"

"What?"

"Bruce, I'm not kidding. She wants a divorce and plans to take my construction company. I hate the bitch. How much does a hit go for these days?"

"Kenny, I have no idea, Vegas isn't as mobbed up as it used to be, and these guys don't exactly advertise."

"Damn... Anyway Bruce, good to hear from you. How are

146

things with you?"

"Well, after listening to your problems, everything is good with me. Isn't there an easier way to solve this?"

"If you can think of something, let me know. Maybe you could talk to one of those shyster brothers of yours."

"Sandra, it's your old friend Bruce, from college, remember me?" "How is it going with you?"

"Of course, I remember you, I've been thinking about you a lot lately."

"So, you finally realized you made the wrong choice all those years ago."

"I don't know about that, but I'd like to see you again. And all in all, I really can't complain."

"Sandra, this is Bruce you're talking to. What do you mean you can't complain? After all, you are a woman, and what about Walt the missionary and perfect husband? Problems in Shangri-la?"

"Wow, my bitter ex-boyfriend. It sounds like one of us complaining women got the best of you and I love it. As far as Walt is concerned, no problems, we just have an agreement that we vacation separately with no questions asked. So next time you're in town, let me know, I'll make a point to be on vacation."

"Luke, Bruce McGimsey. What's up?"

"Bruce, we haven't talked in months, what's shaking?"

"I don't like the way my life is going. Dead-end job, no children, and I am tired of being alone."

"What are you talking about? That new house you built has got to be like Playboy Mansion West. Hell, you're in charge of the cocktail waitresses, right?"

Is this how all guys think? "It ain't like that, those girls are big trouble."

"Oh, come on, Bruce, allow me one little fantasy. It helps me get through the day just dreaming about the life you live."

"Luke, I wanted to ask you, are you happy? Do you like your life?"

"Are you kidding? I've got two kids from my first wife sucking up child support. I got two kids from my current wife, and she already had two kids of her own and of course they

147

despise me. You know, typical brats, you're not my father so fuck off and die."

Like I'm fresh off the boat, I ask, "Isn't that a financial burden?"

"Jeez, Bruce, do you think? That's like asking do married women whine? Of course it's a financial burden. This is my life. I spend eleven or twelve hours a day at a job I hate, mostly because I hate going home worse. I'd stop and drink but I can't afford it. So instead I go home and fight with my wife, usually about money but once in a while about her kids. Oh, yeah, I hate my wife too."

"What about divorce."

"No way, her first husband is a deadbeat and like an idiot I went and adopted her two kids. So I'm stuck. But hey, I feel for you, buddy. You have it rough because it's lonely and boring having to deal with beautiful women every day. Here's the thing. The difference between you and the rest of us is you still got a chance. Maybe you're not happy but at least you're not unhappy. You still got a shot. My life might as well be over."

Now, I also talked with very happy friends whom I envied, but all in all, not that many. No, after my investigation, my mid-life crisis ended. I quit second-guessing the choices I made and decided to just keep reaching for the gusto.

The Idiot Theory

The idiot theory is the premise that God takes care of idiots. On the flip side, if you were born intelligent, then you're on your own and forget about catching any breaks in life. An idiot will find himself getting lucky over and over and over. Now, to a certain extent, I apply the same theory to ugly people. So if you're ugly and stupid, you've really got it made. For sure, the beautiful aspect of all this is, once you wholeheartedly embrace the idiot theory, it will help you get through the perils and trials of life.

For example, if a person gets that promotion instead of you, you just figure of course the idiot caught the break, who else? Or better yet, when your brother makes that long, winding, two-break birdie putt to win all the money on the eighteenth green, you just say to yourself, of course he made the putt, it just proves I'm better looking than he is. See how that works?

On my first craps dealing job, a lady stepped up, rolled eight or nine passes, then called for a rack or chip holder. She wanted to quit a winner before the dice turned cold. So, a new security guard hustled up a chip carrier. Good service, right? Nope, they fired the guy after his shift. The casino manager reasoned if the guard stalled, maybe the lady gets back in the game and hopefully loses back some or all of her winnings. Right now, you think to yourself, what kind of an idiot fires a guy on his first shift just for giving good service? Why not explain to the guard the casino's reasoning? The casino would then save money by not rehiring and retraining a new security guard. The security guard, a young buck of twenty-one years, would have gladly done whatever. I say the casino manager

Bruce McGimsey

overreacted, and worst of all, he kept overreacting till the day he retired.

That same night, my first night dealing, I was a rookie with an extreme case of the jitters. Three hours into my first shift, the pit boss took me off the game and said to me, "This casino needs dealers who can call, 'Seven out, line away.'"

What was he talking about? "I can call that."

"I know you can, you just never do. If you never call losers for the players, house wins, that means you're unlucky. We don't need unlucky dealers who do nothing but lose the house's money."

"Unlucky?"

"Every time you're on the stick, we lose, meaning you're unlucky. And if you stay unlucky, we'll fire you."

Now, I thought this pit boss inched a little over the top with his superstitions, and he wasn't stopping there. "Go in the break room, don't sit down, don't eat, just stand in front of the mirror and practice saying, 'Seven out, line away, new shooter coming up.' Take as long as you want, but don't come back until you've got it down."

In the break room, a few dealers told me to take it seriously. Humiliating? Embarrassing? Of course, but I kept my job. A few weeks later, I watched that same pit boss lay the same shtick on a different dealer. Only this time the newbie ignored the pit boss's orders and ate lunch instead. The pit boss caught him sandwich-handed and fired him, doing his best to belittle him in the process. How's that for a small-time boss playing big shot?

Maybe the lowest thing casinos pull, and they all pull it, is illegally check an employee's background. Since most of Las Vegas employed union workers, union rules only allowed X number of shifts to determine if the employer kept an employee or fired him. Invariably, the hotel, in gathering background information, circumvented the rules to grab this personal information in the small window of opportunity.

So here I am, a restaurant manager in a downtown hotel, when I get the word from security to fire one of my waitresses. They gave no reason why, just that she failed the background check. Security told me to fire her before her twentieth shift, and as long as that happened, per union rules, no questions asked. I followed that rule to the letter and left the termination notice at the time office. She punched out, received the notice, turned in her uniform, and collected her final check, and security escorted her off the premises. The nice thing about this process, you never terminated anyone in person, which meant that you never dealt with all the drama. You usually never even saw the employee again.

Not this time. This time, the young lady came to see me the very next day and wanted answers. She knew she wouldn't be allowed anywhere on the hotel grounds, so she waited for me where I parked, a public parking garage two blocks away. She told me she knew I liked her and that the customers loved her. No one denied that. She brought such a welcome relief from the old, hard-nosed, battle-weary servers who normally worked for us—you know, the twenty-year veterans of the waitress wars.

I explained to her that I wasn't obligated to give her a reason, and that in doing so, I risked my job. But she just kept pressing me until I finally told her she failed her background check.

"Impossible! Listen, I've worked three jobs in my life and got glowing recommendations from all three. I once got caught soliciting a man for sex at a hotel, and pleaded guilty. It was a desperate time in my life, I was just divorced and couldn't feed my baby. I learned a hard lesson, but no way security found out about that, I paid through the nose to have my records legally sealed. My lawyer promised me no employer would ever find out. If the cops gave out that information, they broke the law."

I hemmed, hawed, and stalled, stonewalling her until she finally left, unsatisfied. But I knew what happened. Every casino in town employed a chief of security who was a former Vegas police officer, meaning they knew people downtown, which rendered sealed records worthless. The security chief simply called his downtown connection.

As fate would have it, a couple weeks later, I went downstairs to visit the maitre d' in our gourmet restaurant. With no one in sight and the place not set to open for another hour, I got to nosing around the podium. Sure enough, I stumbled onto a memo from the owner insisting the maitre d' take special care of a particular couple coming in to eat that night. "Treat them to a full food and beverage comp, sky's the limit." She went on to explain that the woman, a police department secretary at the records division, gave us information from time to time that otherwise we could not obtain. Thanks to our security chief's cultivation of this special contact, we were now inside the background-check loop.

Surprised, hardly, I suspected it all along. But I must say it shocked me to read it. What kind of idiot would put this in a memo on hotel letterhead and sign her name to it? I would have thought that an instruction to the maitre d' to burn this letter applied. So what did I do? Looked around, made sure nobody saw me, and then absconded with that memo. I still have it today. Now, just count all the idiots.

One of my favorite stories and an ordeal every Las Vegan goes through is the old air-conditioning nightmare. Sooner or later, your air conditioner will break down during the hottest month of the year. So imagine no air with the temperature consistently topping out at 112 degrees. After about three hours of sitting in your sauna-ized house, when the repairmen finally get to you, you're ready to say, fix it, I don't care about the cost. You even imply there could be a tip if they get it done that day.

Here's what I'm talking about. One day I'm playing out this air conditioning scenario waiting for the repairmen to arrive. A foreman and a co-worker finally arrived, spent forty-five minutes diagnosing the problem, then laid out the total cost of fixing it. The part alone will cost $210. To drive back to the shop and retrieve a new part it will take two to three hours for two men at $90 an hour. "But I'll fudge a little and only charge you $420." Then another two hours to install the part, but by then they'll be into overtime, so figure time-and-a-half for two men, $405 total. The bill amounted to $1035.

Well, fortunately for me, I kept records on my air conditioning unit, so I hustle over to my desk and pull out a full parts and labor warranty. After the foreman briefly inspects the warranty, he nods to his fellow employee and out the door and onto the roof they go. Five minutes later, the foreman knocks on the door and tells me, go ahead and turn the air conditioner on and you're good to go, no charge. No explanation and no signs of embarrassment, they left, with no need for a new part at all. On this one, pretty much everyone in Las Vegas has played the idiot at least once.

Another all-time favorite story. I sat in my General Manager's office at one of the biggest casinos in Las Vegas, where I'd worked for about two years. I needed to go over the food and beverage budget with Terry, the General Manager. Unannounced, the Dragon Lady barges past Terry's secretary right into his office.

Probably every casino in town has its own special version of the Dragon Lady. Typically, a dragon lady is someone who a casino will do whatever it takes to keep her business, yet because of her abrasive nature, every employee in the casino hates her.

Picture then this Dragon Lady, a tiny little Asian woman who has just lost $400,000 in markers on the blackjack tables, all approved by Terry, our GM. Now she wants $100,000 to play the video poker machines. Markers were one thing, no money changed hands, just chips, Monopoly money. Since the Dragon Lady rarely ever won, writing her markers was simple. But when a casino actually loans money, the process gets a lot more involved, and in those days, the video poker machines were cash-only. So here's how the conversation went.

"I want one hundred thousand dollar, now."

"Look it," Terry said, "the hundred-thousand marker will be no problem, but since you want cash, it'll take a while."

"I go next door, I get one hundred thousand dollar in half hour."

"Hey, if you can get a hundred thousand dollars in half an hour, you can hit me."

So the Dragon Lady marches out, and twenty minutes later she's back and plops a hundred grand down on Larry's desk. "Sit, I hit now."

Larry, a former boxer, knew damn well she wanted her pound of flesh, but at best she stood four foot ten and weighed ninety pounds. "You can hit me, but I'm not going to sit down." He figured her feet would have to leave the floor for her to reach his chin, and without her standing on a stable foundation, how bad could it hurt?

She reached back and threw the most ferocious haymaker she could summon, only to have Larry roll with the punch—he turned his chin in the same direction as the punch. She barely touched him, which made her crazy. So while he laughed and looked in my direction, she caught him completely off guard with a solid kick to the groin. Larry went down.

"Okay, now you laugh." She smiled and picked up her $100,000. "I see you tomorrow."

Superficial, shallow, intellectually challenged—no problem, everyone in Vegas is that way. Here I stood in the men's room of one of the premier nightclubs in the city. The bathroom was packed to the gills, elbowroom only, and a waiting line to get to the urinals. So now a guy presently at a urinal yells to his buddy, "Hey, Billy, watch this, I'm going to piss, fart, and burp all at the same time." Then he proceeded to do it. Everyone in the bathroom cheered and applauded in unison including me. What kind of idiot can be impressed by this? Call this an idiot explosion.

D.O.M. Unite

I was food shopping, in that semi-conscious stupor I fall into occasionally, at my neighborhood grocery store. You know, when you stare at something or someone and you don't even realize you're staring because you're in such a daze? Next thing I know, this extremely well endowed hussy in a halter-top walks by me.

Being a typical man, I took one glance lasting no longer than a split second, when the gal turns and says to me, loud enough to be heard in the parking lot, "Aren't these great? I just got them two months ago. If we weren't in this store, I'd let you touch them."

She proceeded to tell me how much they cost, how much she figures to make from them, and how much they have improved her love life. She rendered me speechless. More than that, it astounded me at how familiar this hot little tart got with me, as if I was her regular breast–implant consultant.

Now, picture this fifty-plus-year-old, slightly overweight lady in a colored T-shirt and sweater giving me disdainful looks just like my ex used to before making some useless point. As I walk by her, she takes her sweater and covers up her bust as if my x-ray vision could see through her shirt and bra. Her obvious assumption being I would just love to get an eyeful of her fifty-year-old chest.

"Ooh, you dirty old man," she says.

Well, already a little embarrassed from the brazen young lap dancer wannabe, I felt the need to defend myself. "What are you talking about?"

"Oh, come on, you've been gawking since you got here. I

155

Bruce McGimsey

heard you talking to that girl."

"Lady, who are you kidding? I was minding my own business and she started talking to me." Now, I briefly looked down to focus on mustering up my best disgusted look, then lifted my head, rolled my eyes, stared her in the face. "I did not initiate that convers—"

A teenage girl crashes our party. "Grandma, I can't find the peanuts. Oh, hi, Bruce, how's Queenie?"

Now, like two boxers counterpunching, the old hag briefly looks away, rolls her eyes, and musters up her most disgusted look. "Do you know this guy? What, you hand out candy in the park to teenage girls? You really are a dirty old man."

"Oh no, Grandma," the girl says, "it's not like that at all. His dog Queenie is the cutest dog I've ever seen. He walks her in the park every day."

"Oh, the old dog routine. These perverts use it all the time. I saw it once on '60 Minutes.'"

"Lady, whaddya think, men turn fifty then all of a sudden their sexual tendencies twist up like a pretzel? Just out of nowhere, skinny little teenage girls start looking good to us? Or we start fantasizing about fat little Boy Scouts."

"Bruce! Skinny little teenager?"

"I didn't mean you."

"Megan, don't talk to him. And no, I don't think you become a dirty old man over night, you probably can't even remember when it happened to you."

I looked around and realized our conversation might be getting a little loud. This certainly figured to be the wrong forum for this kind of discussion. At the same time, I hated to let this go. The baseless accusation made me crazy but I realized talking to this witch would just make me angrier.

I did give her one more reproachful look. "Since you fancy yourself such an expert, how does a dirty old man know when he's a dirty old man? I mean, is it an age thing, or are there signs that we're supposed to pick up on? When do you know you've become a dirty old man?"

She looked at me a little perplexed. "That's a good question. But you'd know better than I would."

Once I settled down in my car, I felt proud not to

156

have resorted to name-calling in the store. I liked the granddaughter simply because she treated my dog so well. I also felt I raised an interesting question. How does one know when he has become a dirty old man, and how come you never hear the phrase dirty old woman? When an old woman gets aggressive, it's perceived as cute. Just when does this unflattering pinnacle become a reality during a life? Why did the young tart feel so comfortable talking to me about her refurbished chest? It wasn't like I had dollar bills hanging out of my pockets waiting to tip her.

After all, my sexual inclinations had been the same as early as eight years old, the first time I could recall wondering about it. I remember as a boy, nobody thought it odd to think about sex. In high school, everyone laid it off as hormones. Then in the twenties and thirties, women seemed to accept it like "guys will be guys." Lots of times you came off as weird if you acted differently than the stereotypical horndog. But somewhere between that time and probably about fifty, the perceptions of men change. Do we ask for it, and if so, what are the signs? Does the salesman in the clothes department see you and say, "Oh hello, you know we're having a sale on long overcoats." Part of it might be not adhering to a strict dress code like we used to. Or possibly a sure sign is when the cashier at the store gives you your nineteen dollars change in one-dollar bills and says, "Now you're ready for tonight's action."

I know one thing that consistently happens to me: every time I run into an old high school girlfriend, I walk away from her wondering if I look that bad. Is it wrong to admire and sneak looks at younger women? Do all guys do it, or just dirty old men?

I went to a baseball game, and this gal next to me, probably a stripper, talked to me all night instead of to her date. She told me she liked old guys, they enjoyed life more. It sounded like code for "Hey, without guys like you, girls like me couldn't make a living."

Okay, the encounter with Mrs. Hellfire put my thought processes in overdrive. Maybe I let her insult get the best of me and it behooved me to forget about finding a witchdoctor

157

Bruce McGimsey

in Haiti just to make me a voodoo doll. Besides, I'd need a current photograph of her, and I got tired of lugging my camera to the grocery store.

Three months later, I'm walking Queenie in the park and I run into Megan, her girlfriend Cathy, and two boys trying like crazy to impress them. The girls were eating lunch by the swings, and Megan yelled out, "Hi, Queenie!"

The two boys break out in hysterics. "You call that guy a queen right to his face?"

"No, you idiot, that's his dog's name."

A half dozen little kids were playing together on the slides while their mothers sat at a park table. I waved at the ladies, and Queenie raced toward the kids hoping to entice them into playing fetch with her ball, a daily ritual. As I watched my dog enjoying herself, Megan started screaming, "Bruce, help us, Cathy is choking!"

For a brief second I hesitated, picturing the four of them laughing at me as they yelled "Gotcha!" So I gave Cathy a good look and yelled, "Are you sure?"

"Yes, I'm sure, she's gonna die!"

Cindy, one of the mothers, said, "You gotta do this, Bruce, I don't know how."

So, stepping into high gear, I ran over, lifted Cathy up to a standing position, had her put her arms down by her side, and successfully performed the Heimlich maneuver. A piece of chicken rocketed out of her mouth and crashed landed about five yards away. She took a couple of deep breaths. I looked at her and waited for a big hug and heartfelt thanks for saving her life.

"Jesus Christ, I think you broke my fucking ribs. Did you have to squeeze so hard?"

"You know, it's been years since anyone called me Jesus Christ, and I appreciate the comparison, but trust me, this was not a Jesus-type miracle, just the Heimlich maneuver. In the future, just call me Bruce."

Cindy laughed and told me good job. The two boys looked for kiss points with the girls so they said nothing. Megan appeared to side with Cathy like, shame on you, Bruce. No problem, I felt good about myself—until the next day, that is.

158

As I'm walking Queenie in the park, just like a hurricane brewing out in the ocean, Grandma Bitch lurked about waiting to share some of her wisdom. First thing, she accused me of purposely misconstruing the situation so I could wrap my arms around a defenseless young girl and maybe play on her emotions afterwards.

"I found out how easy it is to pop something out of a windpipe. My friend told me you didn't even have to wrap your arms around her, you could have easily done it with your palm. You really are a dirty old man. If I could, I'd get you banned from this park."

I'd never convince her that I wasn't a dirty old man, so why try? Instead, maybe I could aggravate the hell out of her.

"You know, lady, you got me figured out like a road map. I'm a card-carrying member of the dirty old man's club and president of the Las Vegas chapter."

"You're not serious, there's no such thing."

"Lady, I'm as serious as crack cocaine on Main Street. Tonight we'll kick off our rally at 12 o'clock. Then as the song goes, 'In Numbers Too Big to Ignore,' we're gonna climb up on our rooftops and yell, I love T and A, and I'm not going to hide it anymore."

"Oh, God, you think this is funny, don't you?"

"Lady, my name isn't God, it's Bruce. For the life of me I don't understand why everyone in this park keeps making that mistake. I suppose next you'll want my forgiveness. And yes, I do think this is funny because tomorrow we're gonna meet at the park, come out from behind the bushes, throw away our raincoats, and march lockstep, pockets full of dollar bills, to the hottest strip joint in town."

"Is that right?"

"And by the way, lady, its mister dirty old man to you, and don't call me old."

"By any chance are you the Bruce that went to Las Vegas High School?"

"How did you know?"

"I'm Jody Raddemaker."

"Jody Raddemaker, I don't believe it. I haven't seen you since the ninth grade. How's your mother?"

159

"She's fine. How come you never kept in touch like you promised, we only moved across town."

"Well, you know. What's with the dirty old man stuff?"

"You can't be too careful in today's world. What's with the dirty old man's club, is that true?"

"Of course not, I was just trying to piss you off. Did it work?"

"That's how I recognized you. It sounded just like something you'd say."

"Well, Jody, come on, let's sit down, we've got a lot of catching up to do."

"About thirty-five years worth."

Just Turn and
Face the Monster

"Trick or treat."

"Oh look, honey, it's a ghost. I'm scared. Will you come and give him some candy?"

"Sure, dear. Here you go, buddy."

A faint little voice said, "Thank you, mister, can I have some more?"

"No, kid, now you're being greedy. It's Halloween and I need this candy to last all night. There are a lot of you guys out there." The man then shot a stern look at Oggie, the teenager apparently acting as chaperone for this young toddler dressed in a sheet.

I was seven years old and had looked forward to this night for weeks. The group I trick-or-treated with consisted of my friend Clark, his younger brother Bobby, and the Raddemaker twins, Judy and Jody. We hated being stuck with the twins, but their mother had requested, via my mother, that they accompany us. Since my older brother Jerry, a fifth grader, was assigned as our chaperone, it made Mrs. Raddemaker more comfortable.

Now, right before we head to this upcoming house, Danny Riggs and Oggie, two neighborhood teenagers in high school, walk up and tell us they are going to trick-or-treat with us for the next few houses. So picture the seven of us walking up to the doorstep of this house all looking to get paid, while Jerry and Danny Riggs hold back as chaperones at a distance, Oggie gets down on his knees and puts a sheet over his head. We knew Oggie and Danny from being two of the neighborhood kids, but

161

Bruce McGimsey

I couldn't figure what they were doing in the sheet. Oggie had older brothers well out of high school but no younger siblings. Nonetheless, here was a kid asking for more candy while we stood back from the doorway waiting our turn.

Now Oggie with the awkward sounding voice says, "Jeez, mister, don't be such a fucking cheapskate. Give me some more candy."

The resident goes into tilt mode. "Look, you greedy little bastard, I ain't giving you another thing." He looks at Danny. "You wanna control your little brother here, he's way out of line."

"Hey, I can't control the little jerk," Danny says, "that's just the way he is."

Next thing I know, the sheet comes off, and a six-foot teenager stands up from squatting on his knees. "Okay, Mac, thanks for the candy, but you're still a fucking cheapskate." Then he and Oggie flee the scene in hysterics.

Now, even at our young age, we found this to be funny, and since we couldn't control our laughter, we ended up getting squat from that guy. Still, seeing this seemed well worth it, at least the first couple of times. As we moved down the block, Oggie and Danny performed the same routine over and over.

Understand, Danny Riggs, a junior in high school, maintained the most obnoxious reputation in the neighborhood. I don't think he ever knew the twins' real names, he just called them fatso and chubby. Sure, they were overweight, and they always seemed to be munching on a treat, but they were only six years old. The girls had a cousin Danny's age who lived next door to Oggie. She always referred to Danny as Eddie Haskell, of "Leave It to Beaver" fame. According to her, Danny loved the comparison.

Eventually, the neighborhood hooligans, Danny and Oggie got bored with the same old gag and left, allowing us to focus on candy collection again, an extremely important endeavor for six-and seven-year-olds and not to be taken lightly. Halfway through our quest, it appeared I would fulfill the quota my brother Jerry had set for me.

We had an hour and a half left on my mother's Halloween curfew with our bags already half-full. So as we turned the corner to start a new block, our next victim was Oggie's house. This place's porch sat back away from the street with shrubs and oleanders blocking any view of the front door. Along the other side, a four-foot block wall extended all the way to the street and separated the twins' aunt's place from Oggie's house. Here, Jerry would have to follow us all the way to the door or lose sight of us and wait by the street. If he followed us, one might mistake him to be trick-or-treating, and fifth graders were way too cool for that.

So just imagine our gleeful ecstasy when we arrive at the front door only to find a gigantic bowl chock-full of candy on a table with a sign taped to it reading, "Please, one piece of candy per child." With no apparent grownups about to distribute said candy, we attacked the bowl like hyenas at a zebra kill. We shoved and elbowed, each of us trying to secure the whole bowl.

"Save some for us!" Jody yelled.

"Hey, it's every man for himself!"

Right then, Danny comes out of nowhere, "What the hell are you kids doing? Can't you read, the sign says one piece per kid."

"Holy Toledo, Danny, you scared the crap out of us. Were you hiding behind the bushes this whole time?"

"Yup, and it serves you right, now we're going to have to take our candy back."

"What are you talking about, we hardly got any candy."

Oggie says, "That's because you were trying to hog it all. You had this whole big bowl and you couldn't even share it."

"Hold on, you've taken almost all of our candy."

Danny says, "Well, you little bastard, we can go call your parents and tell them you tried to steal the whole bowl."

"You can't do that," Jody yells, "my mother would spank us!"

What could I say? These two had pulled off the perfect crime. We couldn't even tattle to our parents, we were so ashamed. With nothing but a few tidbits left of our stash, pleading to Jerry for help proved next to useless.

However, simply because my loss was his loss, he devised a plan as to how we could get our candy back. But when it came time to institute his plan, he bugged out. "Hey, I'm not messing with Danny Riggs, that guy spent a year in juvie for biting a kid's ear off. Forget it, I'm going home. You guys are so little he probably won't beat you up." Nobody I knew ever saw this fight or the one-eared loser, but the story scared us all. Heaven knows, I sure believed it.

Jerry chose to go home, but not the rest of us. I had this thing about getting even that would hang with me the rest of my life. We would implement the plan, and who cared what Jerry thought? After all, this was the guy who tormented me for months telling me that the Crinkly Lady lived in a secret passage behind our bedroom closet. So every night before bed, I would secure the closet door with a chair. Then, halfway through the night, I'd wake up to find the chair in the corner and the door wide open. Plus, my table lamp would be unplugged. Months went by before I finally caught Jerry sabotaging my security efforts.

After watching the two teenage numbskulls work the same shtick on a couple other unsuspecting groups, we realized why the candy heaped over the bowl, which only made us more determined. First thing, we unloaded some water balloons from behind the shrubs, nailing the teenage candy crooks and aggravating the hell out of them.

Normally, we'd have no chance to outrun high school kids, but this time we deployed the girls behind the wall that separated Oggie's house from the twins' aunt's. A convenient hose lay across the yard parallel to the cement driveway, obviously placed there for watering purposes by Oggie's parents. So as the boys ran after us, Jody pulled up the hose, tripping them and sprawling them out on the pavement. Meanwhile, Judy, who had snuck into Oggie's backyard, now ran to Oggie's front door and snatched up the whole bowl of loot. Then the twins dashed for the sanctuary of their aunt's house. With both Danny and Oggie lying on the cement pavement, we felt secure fifty yards away.

The only flaw in our plan seemed to be the lack of both foresight and remorse about the two high school kids getting skinned up. As the two of them lay in agony on Oggie's driveway, Danny yelled at us, "I'll get you!"

Little did I know just how mad Danny got. Two days later, Danny and Oggie pulled up to me and the twins walking home from school for lunch. I swear smoke blew out of Danny's ears as he yelled, "Let's see how smart you are now!"

Jody yelled, "Run through the desert, it rained last night!" Since the guys didn't care to get their shoes muddy, I secured a brief reprieve. One thought, now reverberated through my small little head. For the first time, I wondered how I'd look with one ear.

After a few more close calls, my luck ran out one Saturday night. My friend John Goodpasture came to my front door and asked me to come out and play. For a two-dollar bribe, John had sold me out. Once I got outside, Danny snatched me up and took me to Oggie's backyard where Oggie already held Clark and Bobby. I'd been living in such fear, maybe the time had come to just turn and face this monster.

Then again, Clark and Bobby were crying like crazy, and I had no stomach for pain nor the thought of going through life with one ear. Now, in my darkest hour, the makings of a miracle began to transpire.

The Raddemakers' cousin, who also doubled as Danny's classmate, leaned her head out of her back door and yelled, "Hey Danny, your mother phoned and said Fluffy Hughes is trying to find you. She's going to call you back in five minutes."

I didn't know Fluffy Hughes, but these two shot like a rocket for Danny's house. "Fluffy Hughes, what do you think she wants? I'll deal with you squirts later."

Next thing I know, these two go sprawling across the same paved driveway. Jody had jerked the hose again, tripping them with the same trick to the same result.

The front door of the aunt's house flies open, and Jody's cousin and her boyfriend jump out laughing. "Hey, guys, why don't you pick on someone your own size? These kids are seven years old, for Christ sakes." The boyfriend just happened to be headed for USC as a middle linebacker and forewarned Danny to drop this feud with the little guys.

But I'm afraid I never reciprocated the friendship the Raddemakers showed me throughout my childhood. Hell, truth be known, I always wanted to thank Fluffy Hughes, figuring

165

she must have been some looker. It would take me years to truly appreciate the character and class the twins consistently displayed, not just for me but also for probably every friend they ever had.

Occasionally, when visiting my parents, my mother would recommend I call the Raddemaker girls. They had moved across town after ninth grade and I didn't see the twins for thirty-five years. After our chance encounter, Jody and I got together. Maybe I finally grew up enough to look past my tendencies of favoring the outer superficial qualities of a person and try to focus on character and inner beauty. Heaven knows Jody is loaded. And maybe Jody saw qualities in me that nobody else ever saw. I've never been quite sure, but I've been with her for the last few years.

Life is sweet after all.

Bruce McGimsey is a first time author with a unique perspective of the Vegas scene. His Las Vegas experience spans several professions including courier, small business owner, card dealer, and entrepreneur. He even did an impromptu gig as a fortuneteller and impersonator. His natural ability for oral story is in great demand at social gatherings and events in Nevada and surrounding states. This eventually led him to the Henderson Writer's Group and Las Vegas Writer's Conference where he has perfected his writing skills and narrative abilities.

Made in the USA
Middletown, DE
27 February 2023